The Grain Bowl

Nik Williamson

The Grain Bowl

Introduction

Let me start by explaining my interest in grains. In the summer of 2013 I quit my job in finance to start a food business. My knowledge of grain was like that of most people—average—however, due to what I can only describe as fate, I somehow became a bit of an expert on edible grains. The short story is that I was asked to prepare a Scandinavian breakfast for a client. This then led to me deciding to set up a pop-up café called the Porridge Café, a one-month experiment to see if I could share my love of porridge with the world. I began doing lots of recipe testing after the café closed each day, and it served to strengthen my interest in grains, cereals, and seeds—think quinoa, oats, rye, chia, spelt, buckwheat, barley, amaranth, black rice, and millet—and the amazing health benefits they have. We already had thirty dishes on the menu at the café, which was ambitious for such a small project, but I found that this was merely scratching the surface. There was so much potential for grain dishes given the sheer number of different textures and flavors. I was hooked and wanted to explore further.

After geeking out on grains for some time I decided I wanted to show off their potential and encourage others to be creative and adventurous when cooking with them. And so I wrote *The Grain Bowl*. Edible grain is something that has been consumed by human beings since the very beginning of our existence, which might explain why many people find it familiar and comforting when they eat cooked grains for the first time. That bowl food has become very popular in recent times, probably has a lot to do with the convenience of a bowl in the fast pace of city life. It means you can regulate your food intake, since the portion size always remains the same. A bowl of cooked grains or what many call "porridge" is therefore comforting, convenient but also full of exciting possibilities. It can be hot or cold, sweet or savory, indulgent or healthy. If you're not sure what porridge is, then quite simply it's a milled grain, like oats, boiled in water or milk of some kind.

Beyond that you can make it as simple or as fantastically complicated as you like, even using seeds and rice instead of grains (see page 13). Because of its versatile nature it can be eaten for breakfast, lunch, and dinner—to be honest you can eat it whenever you like!

The word porridge is of British heritage and was used for the first time in a cookbook in the sixteenth century. It can also be related to something called "pottage," which resembled soup or stew, that was at its most popular between the ninth and seventeenth centuries. So its roots are more savory, with people using grains to thicken their stews, much like we now use flour to make a roux for gravy. At that time there was also no refined sugar so most dishes were savory. Yet Britain was by no means the only country to have a dish like porridge—almost every country in the world eats it in some form. The main differences are the grains used and the liquid used to boil them in.

In western Europe, a dish called "frumenty" was eaten during the medieval period. It was made from cracked wheat boiled in water or milk and was often served as a side dish to accompany meat, or eaten on its own with a variety of ingredients. A similar, but sweeter dish has been made in Sicily since at least the seventeenth century, using wheat berries boiled with sugar and, in some cases, chocolate. It's seen as a celebration dish and is served on December 13th every year. In Scandinavia and Finland, meanwhile, there are a number of porridge dishes in each of the countries within the region. In Norway there is *gomme*, that uses oats and milk and *rømmegrøt* that's made from wheat flour, cream, milk, butter, and salt. Finland has *helmipuuro*, which uses potato starch and milk, while in Denmark there is *øllebrød*, that's made from rye bread and beer, as well as *rødgrød*, using potato starch and red summer berries, that's served as pudding.

Across the Middle East many dishes resemble porridge. *Harees*, for example, is a lot like frumenty in the sense that it uses cracked wheat and is served as a savory dish. A huge variety of dishes that resemble porridge exist in Africa too, notably *ga'at* from Ethiopia, *konkonte* in Ghana, *obusuma* in Kenya, *pap* in South Africa and *ugali* in much of southern Africa. In all cases it is a dish that is for the people: frugal, easy to make, and nutritious.

Juk or *jook* is a very popular dish across Korea and other east Asian countries, although recipes primarily use rice as opposed to a flaked or cracked grain. Likewise, in China rice is used to make congee, which is somewhere between a risotto, porridge, and soup. This is less popular in Japan, but nonetheless they do eat something called *okayu*, which is a firmer version of a congee and eaten primarily when ill—a bit like a restorative chicken soup in the west. And in India there are two notable dishes, namely *koozh* and *upma*. *Koozh* is a street food dish served in the Tamil region of India and made from millet. *Upma* is made in south India and is made from dry-roasted semolina.

In North America porridge is called "oatmeal," and uses steel-cut or pinhead oats (in Britain oatmeal refers to a number of varieties of prepared oat grains). Also, in North America, there is a dish called "grits," which uses ground maize (corn), known as hominy. This is a more coarsely ground cornmeal when compared to Italian polenta. In Italy, polenta is very popular as a side dish that is used in place of potato mash and is often flavored with meat stock, Parmesan cheese, and herbs. In short, it is fair to say that almost everywhere in the world there is a simple dish resembling porridge. It is an economical, nourishing dish that can be embellished or left very simple. I have only listed a few of the well known dishes but there are many, many more.

In recent years, porridge has had a resurgence in popularity, in part due to a number of scientists heralding it as an important part of a healthy, balanced diet as well as chefs increasing the range of grains and toppings used to make it. At the same time, new brands have tried to bring a modern approach to the sale of grains used to make porridge, focusing on the health benefits and stripping away any unnecessary additives. There are also brands that make myriad alternative milks, like coconut, almond, hazelnut, hemp, rice, and soy. Each has its individual benefits; rice and hemp milks for example are free of allergens like nut milks and are rich in fatty acids and iron. Toppings, like sugar-free and palm-oil-free peanut butter and the ever-increasing powders made from exotic ingredients, like maca root or acai berries, have helped to increase the added health benefits of eating porridge. Within the fitness community porridge is without doubt the most popular dish to start the day off with a boost.

All the grains used in the recipes in the book contain at least 10 percent of the recommended daily intake of fibre, magnesium, phosphorus, manganese, and vitamin B1 (thiamine). Other than oats, they all also contain vitamin B3 (niacin). Other vitamins and minerals spread through the grains are iron, zinc, copper, selenium, vitamin B2 (riboflavin), vitamin B6 (pyridoxine), and vitamin B9 (folic acid). Different grains provide different health benefits, which is why the recipes in *The Grain Bowl* contain a mix. Rolled oats, for example, have marginally less protein than the equivalent weight of chicken breast. Other grains, such as quinoa and amaranth, have become popular in recent years and they too have a high protein content and contain iron and calcium. Another example, buckwheat, contains protein, fibre, magnesium, phosphorus, copper, manganese, and vitamins B2 and B3. By including a mix of grains in each recipe, there is a broad spectrum of vitamins and minerals to be obtained from each dish.

This growing popularity has even resulted in cafés dedicated solely to porridge, popping up in places like New York City and Copenhagen. These cafés showcase just what can be done with this simple dish to make it really exciting both to taste and to look at. As with all modern and popular food, aesthetics plays a significant role in enticing people to try something different and new. Through the medium of social media, chefs have been able to change the perception of porridge by presenting it with flashes of color and different textures, showing its versatility. Instagram, in particular, has served as a place for professionals and amateurs to showcase what they have been making at home or in their restaurant or café. Different trends in presentation have also emerged, with the influence of the Michelin-starred restaurants' methods of presenting food filtering down to the enthusiastic home cook.

But, most importantly, porridge is delicious. If it is cooked properly and flavored with the right ingredients you will never tire of it. Porridge is essentially a blank canvas, so there's endless fun to be had in continually trying different flavors to keep it fresh. I personally eat porridge because I like the routine of cooking the grains and then the creativity of what I can top it with. It's also a really quick filling breakfast or dinner. Texture plays a huge part for me—I don't like mushy porridge that is gloopy and too wet. I like porridge with a bit of bite, like pasta that is al dente. I like it when I can still chew the grains a little. Lots of people will no doubt like their porridge with more liquid and with no bite at all—each to their own—and that all comes down to cooking it a few times to see how you prefer it. Equally there are those who prefer it cold, like bircher muesli. You can soak oats in a fresh juice or one of the many alternative milks, so that you don't have to eat it hot, which is great in the warmer months.

The approach I took when compiling the recipes in the book was to try and be inclusive of all tastes and techniques when using grains to make a bowl of something delicious and nourishing. There are influences from many dishes from around the world. In most cases I wanted to try and bring lots of flavors together and compliment the grains used. Like with most cooking, a recipe only needs to serve as inspiration to create something of your own that you can tailor to your own taste and to help with this, I have started the book with a grain cooking guide (see page 13) so that you can have a perfect base on which to build your own creations. The best thing about food like this is that it can be different every day or be a regular warming and familiar taste.

Grain
Cooking
Guide

Grain Cooking Guide

AMARANTH

COOKING TIME

20 MINUTES

AMARANTH PER PERSON

¼ CUP (2 OZ / 50 G)

LIQUID PER PERSON

1 CUP (8 FL OZ / 250 ML)

METHOD

Put the amaranth into a medium pan,
pour in the liquid, and place over a high
heat. Bring to a boil, reduce to a simmer,
and stir continuously for 15–20 minutes,
or until the mixture thickens to your
preferred viscosity.

BARLEY FLAKES

COOKING TIME

7–8 MINUTES

BARLEY FLAKES PER PERSON

½ CUP (1½–2 OZ / 40–50 G)

LIQUID PER PERSON

1½ CUPS (12 FL OZ / 350 ML)

METHOD

Put the barley into a medium pan, pour
in the liquid, and place over a high heat.
Bring to a boil, reduce to a simmer,
and stir continuously for 7–8 minutes,
or until the mixture thickens to your
preferred viscosity.

PEARLED BARLEY

COOKING TIME

45 MINUTES

PEARLED BARLEY PER PERSON

½ CUP (3 OZ / 80 G)

LIQUID PER PERSON

1¼ CUPS (10 FL OZ / 300 ML)

METHOD

Follow the savory recipes to bring
flavor to the pearled barley.

BLACK RICE

COOKING TIME

35–45 MINUTES

BLACK RICE PER PERSON

¼ CUP (2 OZ / 50G)

LIQUID PER PERSON

1 CUP (8 FL OZ / 250 ML)

METHOD

Put the black rice into a medium pan,
pour in the liquid, and place over a high
heat. Bring to a boil, reduce to a simmer.
Keep checking and occasionally stirring
to prevent it sticking to the pan.

Grain Cooking Guide

BUCKWHEAT

COOKING TIME

20 MINUTES

BUCKWHEAT PER PERSON

½ CUP (3 OZ / 85 G)

LIQUID PER PERSON

1½ CUPS (12 FL OZ / 350ML)

METHOD

Put the buckwheat into a medium pan, pour in the liquid, and place over a high heat. Bring to a boil, reduce to a simmer, and stir continuously for 15–20 minutes, or until the mixture thickens to your preferred viscosity.

KAMUT (KHORASAN) FLAKES

COOKING TIME

7–8 MINUTES

KAMUT PER PERSON

½ CUP (1½–2 OZ / 40–50 G)

LIQUID PER PERSON

2 CUPS (16 FL OZ / 475 ML)

METHOD

Put the kamut into a medium pan, pour in the liquid, and place over a high heat. Bring to a boil, reduce to a simmer, and stir continuously for 7–8 minutes, or until the mixture thickens to your preferred viscosity.

MILLET

COOKING TIME

15–20 MINUTES

MILLET PER PERSON

⅓ CUP (2½ OZ / 65 G)

LIQUID PER PERSON

1 CUP (8 FL OZ / 250 ML)

METHOD

Put the millet into a medium pan, pour in the liquid, and place over a high heat. Bring to a boil, reduce to a simmer, and stir continuously for 15–20 minutes, or until the mixture thickens to your preferred viscosity.

REGULAR ROLLED OATS

COOKING TIME

4–5 MINUTES

ROLLED OATS PER PERSON

½ CUP (2 OZ / 50G)

LIQUID PER PERSON

1½ CUPS (12 FL OZ / 350ML)

METHOD

Put the oats into a medium pan, pour in the liquid, and place over a high heat. Bring to a boil, reduce to a simmer, and stir continuously for 4–5 minutes, or until the mixture thickens to your preferred viscosity.

Grain Cooking Guide

JUMBO OATS

COOKING TIME

7–9 MINUTES

JUMBO OATS PER PERSON

½ CUP (2 OZ / 50 G)

LIQUID PER PERSON

1½ CUPS (12 FL OZ / 350 ML)

METHOD

Put the jumbo oats into a medium pan,
pour in the liquid, and place over a high
heat. Bring to a boil, reduce to a simmer,
and stir continuously for 7–9 minutes,
or until the mixture thickens to your
preferred viscosity.

STEEL-CUT OATS (PINHEAD OATMEAL)

COOKING TIME

20 MINUTES

STEEL-CUT OATS PER PERSON

½ CUP (1½ OZ / 40 G)

LIQUID PER PERSON

1½ CUPS (12 FL OZ / 350 ML)

METHOD

Put the steel-cut oats into a medium pan,
pour in the liquid, and place over a high
heat. Bring to a boil, reduce to a simmer,
and stir continuously for 15–20 minutes,
or until the mixture thickens to your
preferred viscosity.

BLACK, RED, AND WHITE QUINOA

COOKING TIME

20 MINUTES

QUINOA PER PERSON

½ CUP (2 OZ / 50 G)

LIQUID PER PERSON

1¼ CUPS (10 FL OZ / 300 ML)

METHOD

Put the quinoa into a medium pan, pour in the liquid, and place over a high heat. Bring to a boil, reduce to a simmer, and stir continuously for 15–20 minutes, or until the mixture thickens to your preferred viscosity.

RYE FLAKES

COOKING TIME

7–8 MINUTES

RYE FLAKES PER PERSON

½ CUP (1½–2 OZ / 40–50 G)

LIQUID PER PERSON

1½ CUPS (12 FL OZ / 350 ML)

METHOD

Put the rye flakes into a medium pan, pour in the liquid, and place over a high heat. Bring to a boil, reduce to a simmer, and stir continuously for 7–8 minutes, or until the mixture thickens to your preferred viscosity.

Grain Cooking Guide

SPELT FLAKES

COOKING TIME

7–8 MINUTES

SPELT FLAKES PER PERSON

½ CUP (1½–2 OZ / 40–50 G)

LIQUID PER PERSON

1½ CUPS (12 FL OZ / 350ML)

METHOD

Put the spelt flakes into a medium pan, pour in the liquid, and place over a high heat. Bring to a boil, reduce to a simmer, and stir continuously for 7–8 minutes, or until the mixture thickens to your preferred viscosity.

FARRO (PEARLED SPELT)

COOKING TIME

25 MINUTES

FARRO PER PERSON

½ CUP (3 OZ / 80 G)

LIQUID PER PERSON

1¼ CUPS (10 FL OZ / 300 ML)

METHOD

Follow the savory recipes in the following chapters to allow the grain to absorb the most flavor.

WHEAT FLAKES

COOKING TIME

7–8 MINUTES

WHEAT FLAKES PER PERSON

½ CUP (1½–2 OZ / 40–50 G)

LIQUID PER PERSON

1½ CUPS (12 FL OZ / 350ML)

METHOD

Put the wheat flakes into a medium pan, pour in the liquid, and place over a high heat. Bring to a boil, reduce to a simmer, and stir continuously for 7–8 minutes, or until the mixture thickens to your preferred viscosity.

SOME COOKING NOTES

PORTION SIZE

If you are making straight oat-based porridge or a mix of various grains, the portion size for a filling breakfast once cooked is 1–1½ cups (7–9 oz / 200–250 g). This does not include the topping.

SOAKING VERSUS NOT SOAKING

For me, the end result in taste is the same, however, soaking in a liquid can reduce the cooking time for grains like oats, rye, wheat, and barley flakes. This is due to the grain absorbing the liquid before cooking.

An hour before cooking should be enough time to get a substantial amount of liquid into the grain. You should soak the the grain in the amount of liquid shown in the recipe, cover, and refrigerate. You may find you need to add a little more liquid to the pan once the grain starts to cook compared to a non-soaked grain.

Healthy Sweet Bowls

Barley and Rye with Papaya, Apple, and Chia Seeds

Put the barley flakes, rye flakes, and ½ tablespoon chia seeds into a medium pan, pour in the coconut milk beverage and 1½ cups (12 fl oz / 350 ml) water and place over high heat. Bring to a boil.

Once the liquid has begun to reduce, stir quickly to prevent the porridge from sticking. Cook for 7–8 minutes over medium-high heat, or until the porridge reaches the desired consistency, then remove from the heat.

Divide the porridge between 2 bowls. Top with the apple and papaya, drizzle with the honey and sprinkle with the remaining chia seeds.

SERVES 2
PREPARATION 5 MIN
COOKING 10 MIN

½ CUP (2 OZ / 50 G) BARLEY FLAKES
½ CUP (2 OZ / 50 G) RYE FLAKES
½ TABLESPOON CHIA SEEDS, PLUS
  2 TEASPOONS FOR SPRINKLING
1½ CUPS (12 FL OZ / 350 ML)
  COCONUT MILK BEVERAGE
1 APPLE, CORED AND THINLY SLICED
½ RIPE PAPAYA, PEELED AND
  FINELY DICED
2 TABLESPOONS HONEY

Oats with Banana, Peanut Butter, and Blueberries

Put the oats into a medium pan. Pour in the almond milk and 1½ cups (12 fl oz/350 ml) water and place over high heat. Bring to a boil.

Once the liquid has begun to reduce, stir quickly to prevent the porridge from sticking. Cook for 5 minutes over medium heat, or until the porridge reaches the desired consistency, then remove from the heat.

Divide the porridge between 2 bowls. Top with the banana slices, peanut butter, and blueberries. Drizzle with maple syrup and sprinkle with sea buckthorn powder, if using.

SERVES 2
PREPARATION 2 MIN
COOKING 5 MIN

1 CUP (3½ OZ / 100 G) ROLLED OATS
1½ CUPS (12 FL OZ / 350 ML)
  ALMOND MILK
1 BANANA, SLICED
2 TABLESPOONS SUGAR-FREE AND
  PALM-OIL-FREE PEANUT BUTTER
½ CUP (3 OZ / 80 G) BLUEBERRIES
  (FRESH OR DRIED)
2 TABLESPOONS MAPLE SYRUP
  (OPTIONAL)
½ TEASPOON SEA BUCKTHORN
  POWDER (OPTIONAL)

Amaranth, Kamut, and Oats with Espresso, Walnuts, and Raw Cacao

Put the amaranth into a medium pan. Pour in the almond milk and 1¼ cups (10 fl oz / 300 ml) water and place over high heat. Bring to a boil, then reduce the heat to low and simmer, covered, for 15 minutes.

Add the oats and kamut flakes and increase the heat to medium. Once almost all the liquid has been absorbed, add 1 shot of coffee and stir until the porridge reaches the desired consistency. Remove from the heat.

Divide the porridge between 2 bowls. Top with the banana slices and walnuts and sprinkle with the cacao nibs. Finally, pour over the remaining espresso and the honey.

SERVES 2
PREPARATION 5 MIN
COOKING 22 MIN

⅓ CUP (2¼ OZ / 60 G) AMARANTH
1½ CUPS (12 FL OZ / 350 ML)
  ALMOND MILK
⅓ CUP (1¼ OZ / 30 G) ROLLED OATS
⅓ CUP (1¼ OZ / 30 G) KAMUT FLAKES
2 X 1 FL OZ / 30 ML SHOTS ESPRESSO
  OR 2 X 1 FL OZ / 30 ML SHOT
  GLASSES OF HOT COFFEE
1 BANANA, THINLY SLICED
½ CUP (2¼ OZ / 60 G) WALNUTS
4 TABLESPOONS RAW CACAO NIBS
2 TABLESPOONS HONEY

Buckwheat and Oats with Gooseberries, Black Currants, and Ginger

Put the buckwheat into a medium pan, pour in the coconut milk beverage and 1½ cups (12 fl oz / 350 ml) water and place over medium heat. Cover and bring to a low simmer.

After 15 minutes, add the oats and, if necessary, ½ cup (4 fl oz / 120 ml) water. Cook for 5 minutes, or until the porridge reaches the desired consistency, then remove from the heat. Stir in the grated ginger.

Add the black currants to a small pan with 2 tablespoons water and the stevia or sugar. Place over low heat for a few minutes to soften the fruit.

Divide the porridge between 2 bowls and top with the gooseberries and black currants. Scatter the seeds around the fruit, then drizzle with any remaining black currant juices and the honey to serve.

SERVES 2
PREPARATION 3 MIN
COOKING 25 MIN

½ CUP (2 OZ / 50 G) BUCKWHEAT
1½ CUPS (12 FL OZ / 350 ML) COCONUT
  MILK BEVERAGE
½ CUP (2 OZ / 50 G) ROLLED OATS
2 TEASPOONS FINELY GRATED
  FRESH GINGER
½ CUP (2¾ OZ / 70 G) RIPE GOOSEBERRIES
½ CUP (2 OZ / 50 G) BLACK CURRANTS
1 TEASPOON STEVIA OR 2 TEASPOONS
  SUPERFINE (CASTER) SUGAR
2 TABLESPOONS MIX OF TOASTED
  SUNFLOWER AND PUMPKIN SEEDS
2 TABLESPOONS HONEY

Black Rice and Oats with Mango, Passion Fruit, and Coconut

Put the black rice into a medium pan. Pour in the coconut milk beverage and 1½ cups (12 fl oz / 350 ml) water and place over high heat. Bring to a boil, then reduce the heat to low and simmer, covered, for 35–40 minutes.

Add the oats and increase the heat to medium. Cook, stirring, for 5 minutes, or until the porridge reaches the desired consistency. Remove from the heat and divide the porridge between 2 bowls.

Cut the passion fruit in half and scoop out the pulp. Top the porridge with the mango and passion fruit pulp. Sprinkle with coconut, squeeze over some lime juice, and drizzle with the agave nectar to serve.

SERVES 2
PREPARATION 2 MIN
COOKING 42–47 MIN

¼ CUP (2 OZ / 50 G) BLACK RICE
1 CUP (8 FL OZ / 250 ML) COCONUT
  MILK BEVERAGE
½ CUP (2 OZ / 50 G) ROLLED OATS
1 PASSION FRUIT
½ MANGO, DICED
2 TABLESPOONS GRATED FRESH,
  OR DRY SHREDDED (DESICCATED),
  COCONUT
1 LIME
2 TABLESPOONS AGAVE NECTAR

Barley and Wheat with Blueberries, Lychees, and Pistachios

Put the barley flakes and wheat flakes into a medium pan, pour in the coconut milk beverage and 1½ cups (12 fl oz / 350 ml) water and place over high heat. Bring to a boil.

Once the liquid has begun to reduce, stir quickly to prevent the porridge from sticking. Reduce the heat to medium-high and cook for 7–8 minutes or until the porridge reaches the desired consistency. Remove from the heat.

Divide the porridge between 2 bowls. Top with the blueberries and lychees. Sprinkle with the pistachios and pumpkin seeds, then drizzle with the honey to serve.

SERVES 2
PREPARATION 15 MIN
COOKING 7–8 MIN

½ CUP (2 OZ / 50 G) BARLEY FLAKES
½ CUP (2 OZ / 50 G) WHEAT FLAKES
1½ CUPS (12 FL OZ / 350 ML) COCONUT
  MILK BEVERAGE
½ CUP (3 OZ / 80 G) FRESH OR
  FROZEN BLUEBERRIES
10 LYCHEES, PEELED AND HALVED
  (SEEDS DISCARDED)
4 TABLESPOONS PISTACHIOS, SHELLED
  AND COARSELY CHOPPED
2 TABLESPOONS PUMPKIN SEEDS
2 TABLESPOONS HONEY

Put the oats, wheat flakes, and rye flakes into a medium pan, pour in the coconut milk beverage and 1½ cups (12 fl oz / 350 ml) water and place over high heat. Bring to a boil.

Once the liquid has begun to reduce, stir quickly to prevent the porridge from sticking. Reduce the heat to medium-high and cook for 7–8 minutes, or until the porridge reaches the desired consistency. Remove from the heat.

Stir in the elderflower cordial and divide the porridge between 2 bowls. Top with the raspberries and blueberries and scatter over the goji berries, cacao nibs, coconut, and pumpkin seeds. Drizzle with the honey to serve.

Oats, Wheat, and Rye with Elderflower, Raspberries, and Blueberries

SERVES 2
PREPARATION 5 MIN
COOKING 7–8 MIN

½ CUP (2 OZ / 50 G) ROLLED OATS
¼ CUP (1 OZ / 25 G) WHEAT FLAKES
¼ CUP (1 OZ / 25 G) RYE FLAKES
1½ CUPS (12 FL OZ / 350 ML)
  COCONUT MILK BEVERAGE
2 TABLESPOONS ELDERFLOWER
  CORDIAL
½ CUP (2½ OZ / 65 G) RASPBERRIES
½ CUP (3 OZ / 80 G) BLUEBERRIES
2 TEASPOONS GOJI BERRIES
2 TEASPOONS RAW CACAO NIBS
2 TEASPOONS GRATED FRESH
  OR SHREDDED (DESICCATED)
  COCONUT
2 TEASPOONS PUMPKIN SEEDS
2 TABLESPOONS HONEY

Oats with Ricotta, Caramelized Peach, and Brazil Nuts

Put the oats into a medium pan, pour in the coconut milk beverage and 1½ cups (12 fl oz / 350 ml) water and place over medium heat. Bring to a simmer, cover, and cook for 20 minutes.

Meanwhile, cut the peach in half, remove the pit (stone), and slice each half into 6 pieces. Combine the sugar, salt, and cinnamon in a bowl, add the peach slices, and toss to coat. Heat a nonstick pan over medium-high heat, add the peach slices, and cook for 3–4 minutes, turning every 30 seconds.

In another bowl whisk the ricotta with the vanilla for a couple of minutes. Set aside.

Once the porridge is cooked, remove from the heat and divide between 2 bowls. Top with the ricotta and peach slices. Sprinkle with the Brazil nuts and drizzle with the caramelized liquid left in the pan to serve.

SERVES 2
PREPARATION 4 MIN
COOKING 20 MIN

½ CUP (3 OZ / 80 G) STEEL-CUT
  OATS (PINHEAD OATMEAL)
1½ CUPS (12 FL OZ / 350 ML) COCONUT
  MILK BEVERAGE
1 PEACH
1 TABLESPOON LIGHT BROWN SUGAR
PINCH OF SALT
PINCH OF GROUND CINNAMON
¼ CUP (2¼ OZ / 60 G) FRESH
  RICOTTA CHEESE
1 TEASPOON VANILLA BEAN PASTE
¼ CUP (1 OZ / 25 G) BRAZIL NUTS,
  COARSELY CHOPPED

Quinoa and Oats with Yogurt, Raspberries, and Hazelnuts

Put the quinoa into a medium pan, pour in the almond milk and 1 cup (8 fl oz / 250ml) water and place over high heat. Bring to a boil, then reduce the heat to low and simmer, covered, for 15 minutes.

Add the oats and increase the heat to medium. Cook, stirring, for 5 minutes, or until the porridge reaches the desired consistency. You may need to add up to ½ cup (4 fl oz / 120 ml) more water if the quinoa absorbs too much liquid. Remove from the heat.

Meanwhile, put the raspberries into a small pan, drizzle with 2 tablespoons of the honey, and gently toss with a spoon to coat. Place over low heat and cook lightly for 3 minutes. Remove from the heat.

Divide the porridge between 2 bowls. Top with the yogurt and raspberries and sprinkle with the chopped hazelnuts. Drizzle with the remaining honey and serve.

SERVES 2
PREPARATION 2 MIN
COOKING 22 MIN

⅓ CUP (2½ OZ / 65 G) QUINOA
1 CUP (8 FL OZ / 250 ML) ALMOND
  OR HAZELNUT MILK
½ CUP (2 OZ / 50 G) ROLLED OATS
1 CUP (3½ OZ / 100 G) RASPBERRIES
4 TABLESPOONS HONEY
½ CUP (4 OZ / 120 G) WHOLE
  (FULL-FAT) YOGURT
4 TABLESPOONS CHOPPED HAZELNUTS

Wheat, Rye, and Spelt with Poached Pear, Blackberries, and Apricots

Put the sugar, cinnamon, lemon zest, vanilla, and ginger into a small pan big enough to hold the pear halves. Half-fill the pan with water and bring to a boil. Simmer for 10 minutes to infuse the water with the spices, add the pear halves, cover, and gently poach for 30 minutes, or until soft. If using dried apricots, add them to the pan after 15 minutes. Remove from the heat and set aside.

Put the wheat flakes, rye flakes, and spelt flakes into a medium pan, pour in the coconut milk beverage and 1½ cups (12 fl oz / 350 ml) water and place over high heat. Bring to a boil. Once the liquid has begun to reduce, stir quickly to prevent the porridge from sticking. Reduce to medium-high heat and cook for 7–8 minutes, or until the porridge reaches the desired consistency, then remove from the heat.

Divide the porridge between 2 bowls. Top with the pear halves, blackberries, and apricot slices. Drizzle with the honey and spoon on the yogurt, if using.

SERVES 2
PREPARATION 2 MIN
COOKING 40 MIN

½ CUP (3¾ OZ / 110 G) SUPERFINE
   (CASTER) SUGAR
1 TEASPOON GROUND CINNAMON
2 STRIPS LEMON ZEST (LENGTH OF
   A LEMON, USING A PEELER)
½ TEASPOON VANILLA BEAN PASTE
1 INCH (2.5 CM) PIECE FRESH
   ROOT GINGER, PEELED
1 RIPE PEAR, HALVED LENGTHWISE
⅓ CUP (1¼ OZ / 35 G) WHEAT FLAKES
⅓ CUP (1¼ OZ / 35 G) RYE FLAKES
⅓ CUP (1¼ OZ / 35 G) SPELT FLAKES
1½ CUPS (12 FL OZ / 350 ML)
   COCONUT MILK BEVERAGE
½ CUP (2¼ OZ / 60 G) BLACKBERRIES
1 RIPE APRICOT OR 2 DRIED, SLICED
2 TABLESPOONS HONEY (OPTIONAL)
2 TABLESPOONS GREEK YOGURT
   (OPTIONAL)

Oats with Peanut Butter, Chocolate Truffle, and Banana

Put the oats and the truffles into a medium pan, pour in the almond milk and 1½ cups (12 fl oz / 350 ml) water and place over high heat. Bring to a boil.

Once the liquid has begun to reduce, stir quickly to prevent the porridge from sticking. Reduce to medium-high heat and cook for 5 minutes, or until the porridge reaches the desired consistency, then remove from the heat.

Divide between 2 bowls. Top with the banana slices and peanut butter. Sprinkle with the flaked almonds to serve.

SERVES 2
PREPARATION 2 MIN
COOKING 5 MIN

1 CUP (4 OZ / 125 G) ROLLED OATS
4–6 BITTERSWEET (DARK) CHOCOLATE
   TRUFFLES (MINIMUM 70% CACAO
   CONTENT)
1½ CUPS (12 FL OZ / 350 ML)
   ALMOND MILK
1 BANANA, THINLY SLICED
2 TEASPOONS PEANUT BUTTER
2 TABLESPOONS TOASTED
   FLAKED ALMONDS

Use a peeler to create carrot shavings. Heat a skillet (frying pan) over medium heat, then add the carrot shavings and maple syrup. Allow to caramelize for about 2 minutes, then remove from the heat and set aside.

Put the oats into a medium pan, pour in the coconut milk beverage and 1½ cups (12 fl oz / 350 ml) water and place over high heat. Bring to a boil.

Once the liquid has begun to reduce, stir quickly to prevent the porridge from sticking. Reduce to medium-high heat and cook for 20 minutes, or until the porridge reaches the desired consistency. Stir in the grated zucchini (courgette) and cook for 1 minute, then remove from the heat.

Divide the porridge between 2 bowls. Top with the orange rounds, walnuts, caramelized carrot shavings, and seeds to serve.

Oats with Caramelized Carrots, Zucchini, and Walnuts

SERVES 2
PREPARATION 5 MIN
COOKING 25 MIN

1 CARROT, ORGANIC IF POSSIBLE
1 TEASPOON MAPLE SYRUP
1 CUP (3½ OZ / 100 G) ROLLED OATS
1½ CUPS (12 FL OZ / 350 ML)
  COCONUT MILK BEVERAGE
1 SMALL ZUCCHINI (COURGETTE),
  FINELY GRATED
1 ORANGE, PEELED AND SLICED
  INTO ROUNDS
2 TABLESPOONS WALNUTS
2 TABLESPOONS MIXED SEEDS (PUMPKIN,
  SUNFLOWER, CHIA, SESAME)

Oats and Rye with Baked Plums, Cherries, and Pickled Hazelnuts

SERVES 2
PREPARATION 5 MIN, PLUS
MARINATING OVERNIGHT
COOKING 25 MIN

½ CUP (1 OZ / 25 G) HAZELNUTS
6 TABLESPOONS (3 FL OZ /
   90 ML) APPLE CIDER VINEGAR
1 TABLESPOON STEVIA, PLUS
   1 TEASPOON TO SPRINKLE, OR
   2 TABLESPOONS SUPERFINE
   (CASTER) SUGAR, PLUS
   2 TEASPOONS TO SPRINKLE
1 STAR ANISE
½ TEASPOON GROUND CINNAMON
2 PLUMS
2 TABLESPOONS MAPLE SYRUP
½ CUP (2¼ OZ / 60 G) CHERRIES,
   HALVED AND PITTED (STONED)
½ CUP (2 OZ / 50 G) ROLLED OATS
½ CUP (2 OZ / 50 G) RYE FLAKES
1½ CUPS (12 FL OZ / 350 ML)
   ALMOND MILK
1 TABLESPOON HONEY

Put the hazelnuts into a small pan, add ⅔ cup (5 fl oz / 150 ml) water, the vinegar, stevia or sugar, star anise, and cinnamon and place over low heat. Bring to a simmer and cook for 10 minutes. Strain the liquid into a bowl. Chop the hazelnuts and return to the liquid. Once cool, chill in the refrigerator overnight.

Preheat the oven to 350°F/180°C/Gas Mark 4.

Cut the plums in half, remove and discard the pits (stones). Put the plum halves into an ovenproof bowl and coat with maple syrup. Cook in the oven for 15 minutes, or until the plums are soft but not falling apart.

Meanwhile, put the cherries into a bowl and sprinkle with the stevia or sugar. Leave to macerate while the plums are cooking.

Put the oats and rye flakes in a medium pan, pour in the almond milk and 1½ cups (12 fl oz / 350 ml) water and place over high heat. Bring to a boil. Once the liquid has begun to reduce, stir quickly to prevent the porridge from sticking. Reduce to medium-high heat and cook for 7–8 minutes, or until the porridge reaches the desired consistency, then remove from the heat.

Divide the porridge between 2 bowls. Top with the plum halves and macerated cherries and scatter over the pickled hazelnuts. Drizzle with any leftover liquid from the plums and cherries, along with the honey to serve.

Millet and Oats with 3-Berry Compote, Banana, and Seeds

Put the millet into a medium pan, pour in the coconut milk beverage and 1½ cups (12 fl oz / 350 ml) water. Place over high heat. Bring to a boil, then reduce the heat to low and simmer, covered, for 15–17 minutes.

Meanwhile, make the compote. Put all the berries into a small pan, add 2 tablespoons of the honey and 1 tablespoon water. Place over medium–low heat for 5 minutes, until the berries start to soften and the honey is absorbed. The fruit should be soft but still retain some of its shape.

Add the oats to the millet and increase the heat to medium. Cook, stirring, for 7–8 minutes, or until the porridge reaches the desired consistency, then remove from the heat. You may need to add a little more milk if the millet absorbs too much liquid.

Divide the porridge between 2 bowls. Top with the berry compote and banana slices, and sprinkle with the flaxseed (linseed). Drizzle with the remaining honey to serve.

SERVES 2
PREPARATION 2 MIN
COOKING 25 MIN

½ CUP (3½ OZ / 100 G) MILLET
1½ CUPS (12 FL OZ / 350 ML) COCONUT
  MILK BEVERAGE
1 CUP (3½ OZ / 100 G) MIX OF
  RASPBERRIES, BLACKBERRIES, AND
  STRAWBERRIES, HULLED
4 TABLESPOONS HONEY
½ CUP (2 OZ / 50 G) ROLLED OATS
1 BANANA, SLICED
2 TEASPOONS FLAXSEED (LINSEED)

Quinoa and Oats with Rhubarb, and Almond Brittle

SERVES 2
PREPARATION 3 MIN,
PLUS COOLING
COOKING 35 MIN

1 STICK OF RHUBARB, CHOPPED INTO
   1½ INCH (4 CM) LENGTHS
½ TEASPOON STEVIA OR 2 TEASPOONS
   SUPERFINE (CASTER) SUGAR
2 TEASPOONS BUTTER
4 TEASPOONS SUPERFINE
   (CASTER) SUGAR
PINCH OF SALT
3 TABLESPOONS TOASTED
   FLAKED ALMONDS
1 TEASPOON VERY FINELY CHOPPED
   GINGER PRESERVES (PRESERVED
   GINGER IN SYRUP), OPTIONAL
3 TABLESPOONS ORGANIC YOGURT
   (OPTIONAL)
⅓ CUP (2¼ OZ / 60 G) QUINOA
1½ CUPS (12 FL OZ / 350 ML)
   ALMOND MILK
½ CUP (2 OZ / 50 G) ROLLED OATS
2 TABLESPOONS HONEY

Preheat the oven to 350°F/180°C/Gas Mark 4. Line a small plate with parchment (baking) paper.

Put the rhubarb into a small ovenproof dish, sprinkle with the stevia or sugar, toss, then shuffle the rhubarb so the pieces form a single layer. Cook in the oven for 15 minutes, or until the rhubarb is soft but not completely falling apart. Remove from the heat and set aside.

Meanwhile, put the butter, sugar, and salt into a small pan and place over medium heat. Allow to bubble until it turns golden brown but not burned. Add the flaked almonds and stir to coat them in the mixture. Transfer to the lined plate and allow to cool completely.

If using, mix the preserved ginger into the yogurt; alternatively use a blender. Set aside.

Put the quinoa into a medium pan, pour in the almond milk and 1½ cups (12 fl oz / 350 ml) water and place over medium heat. Bring to a simmer, cover, and cook for about 15 minutes. Add the oats and increase to medium-high heat. You may need to add up to ¼ cup (2 fl oz / 60 ml) more water if most of the liquid has been absorbed. Cook, stirring, for 5 minutes, or until the porridge reaches the desired consistency, then remove from the heat.

Divide the porridge between 2 bowls. Top with the almond brittle and rhubarb pieces, then add the ginger yogurt, if using. Drizzle with the honey to serve.

Rye and Oats with Apple, Rhubarb, and Cinnamon

Put the rhubarb into a small pan and pour in just enough water to cover. Bring to a simmer and add the stevia or sugar. Cook gently over medium-low heat for 10 minutes, or until the rhubarb is soft but not completely falling apart.

Meanwhile, put the rye flakes into a medium pan, pour in the almond milk and 1½ cups (12 fl oz / 350 ml) water and place over high heat. Bring to a boil. Reduce to medium-high heat and cook for 5 minutes. Add the oats and cook, stirring, for 5–8 minutes, or until the porridge reaches the desired consistency. Remove from the heat.

Dry-fry the seeds in a skillet (frying pan) over medium heat, stirring frequently, for 2 minutes. Do not allow them to burn.

Stir 1 teaspoon of the cinnamon into the rye and oats before dividing the porridge between 2 bowls. Top with the apple slices, spoon over the hot rhubarb, then sprinkle with the seeds and remaining cinnamon. Drizzle with the honey to serve.

SERVES 2
PREPARATION 10 MIN
COOKING 15 MIN

2 STICKS OF RHUBARB, CHOPPED INTO
  ¾ INCH (2 CM) LENGTHS
1 TEASPOON STEVIA OR 2 TEASPOONS
  SUPERFINE (CASTER) SUGAR
½ CUP (2 OZ / 50 G) RYE FLAKES
1½ CUPS (12 FL OZ / 350 ML)
  ALMOND MILK
½ CUP (2 OZ / 50 G) REGULAR OATS
2 TABLESPOONS MIX OF SUNFLOWER,
  PUMPKIN, AND FLAXSEED (LINSEED)
1 APPLE, CORED AND THINLY SLICED
2 TEASPOONS GROUND CINNAMON
2 TABLESPOONS HONEY

Preheat the oven to 350°F/180°C/Gas Mark 4.

Put the nectarine halves cut-side up on a baking sheet lined with parchment (baking) paper. Bake for 15 minutes until soft.

Meanwhile, put the quinoa into a medium pan, pour in the almond milk and 1 cup (8 fl oz / 250 ml) water and place over medium heat. Bring to a simmer, cover, and cook for 15 minutes.

Add the oats and kamut flakes to the quinoa and cook, stirring, for 10 minutes, or until the porridge reaches the desired consistency. You may need to add up to ¼ cup (2 fl oz / 60 ml) more water if the quinoa absorbs too much liquid. Remove from the heat.

Stir 1 teaspoon of the cinnamon into the porridge, then divide it between 2 bowls. Top with the nectarine halves, then sprinkle with the raspberries, black grapes, and chia seeds. Dust with the remaining cinnamon and drizzle with the honey to serve.

Quinoa, Oats, and Kamut with Baked Nectarine, Raspberries, and Black Grapes

SERVES 2
PREPARATION 5 MIN
COOKING 25 MIN

1 NECTARINE, HALVED AND
  PITTED (STONED)
¼ CUP (1½ OZ / 40 G) QUINOA
1½ CUPS (12 FL OZ / 350 ML)
  ALMOND MILK
⅓ CUP (1¼ OZ / 30 G) ROLLED OATS
⅓ CUP (1¼ OZ / 30 G) KAMUT FLAKES
2 TEASPOONS GROUND CINNAMON
½ CUP (2½ OZ / 65 G) RASPBERRIES
½ CUP (3 OZ / 80 G) BLACK GRAPES,
  HALVED AND SEEDED
2 TEASPOONS CHIA SEEDS
2 TABLESPOONS HONEY

Oats and Millet with Mango, Figs, and Lime

Put the oats and millet into a medium pan, pour in the coconut milk beverage and 1½ cups (12 fl oz / 350 ml) water and place over medium heat. Bring to a simmer, cover, and cook for 20 minutes.

In a small bowl, mix the lime zest and stevia or sugar and set aside.

Divide the porridge between 2 bowls. Top with the mango and fig slices, sprinkle with the lime zest mixture and the coconut, then drizzle with the honey to serve.

SERVES 2
PREPARATION 5 MIN
COOKING 20 MIN

½ CUP (1½ OZ / 40 G) STEEL-CUT OATS
  (PINHEAD OATMEAL)
1 CUP (3½ OZ / 100 G) MILLET
1½ CUPS (12 FL OZ / 350 ML) COCONUT
  MILK BEVERAGE
GRATED ZEST OF 1 LIME
½ TEASPOON STEVIA OR 1 TEASPOON
  SUPERFINE (CASTER) SUGAR
½ MANGO, THINLY SLICED
2 FIGS, THINLY SLICED
2 TEASPOONS GRATED FRESH
  OR DRY SHREDDED (DESICCATED)
  COCONUT
2 TABLESPOONS HONEY

Quinoa and 5-Grains with Acai Berries, Banana, and Apricots

Leave the acai berry pulp to thaw at room temperature.

Put the quinoa into a medium pan, pour in the coconut milk beverage and 1½ cups (12 fl oz / 350 ml) water and place over medium heat. Bring to a simmer, cover, and cook for 15 minutes.

Add the remaining grains to the pan and increase the heat to medium-high. You may need to add up to ¼ cup (2 fl oz / 60 ml) water if most of the liquid has been absorbed.

Cook, stirring, for 7 minutes or until the porridge reaches the desired consistency. Remove from the heat and stir in half the acai berry pulp.

Divide the porridge between 2 bowls. Top with the remaining acai berry pulp and the banana and apricot slices. Sprinkle with the goji berries and chia seeds, and drizzle with the honey to serve.

SERVES 2
PREPARATION 2 MIN, PLUS THAWING
COOKING 22 MIN

3½ OZ / 100 G FROZEN ORGANIC
  ACAI BERRY PULP
⅓ CUP (2¼ OZ / 60 G) QUINOA
1½ CUPS (12 FL OZ / 350 ML) COCONUT
  MILK BEVERAGE
½ CUP (2 OZ / 50 G) MIX OF ROLLED
  OATS, RYE FLAKES, WHEAT FLAKES,
  BARLEY FLAKES AND SPELT FLAKES
1 BANANA, SLICED
1 APRICOT, HALVED, PITTED (STONED),
  AND THINLY SLICED
2 TEASPOONS GOJI BERRIES
2 TEASPOONS CHIA SEEDS
2 TABLESPOONS HONEY

Oats, Buckwheat, and Millet with Blood Orange, Carrot, and Cardamom

Put the oats, buckwheat, and millet into a medium pan, pour in the coconut milk beverage and 1½ cups (12 fl oz / 350 ml) water and place over medium heat. Bring to a simmer, cover, and cook for 20 minutes.

Use a vegetable peeler to peel thin strips from 1 carrot. Finely grate the other carrot. Set aside.

Stir the cardamom and ginger into the porridge and divide between 2 bowls. Top with the grated carrot, carrot strips, blood orange segments, and walnuts. Spoon the mascarpone onto each each bowl, if using, and drizzle with the honey to serve.

SERVES 2
PREPARATION 5 MIN
COOKING 20 MIN

½ CUP (1½ OZ / 40 G) STEEL-CUT OATS
  (PINHEAD OATMEAL)
¼ CUP (1 OZ / 25 G) BUCKWHEAT
¼ CUP (2 OZ / 50 G) MILLET
1½ CUPS (12 FL OZ / 350 ML) COCONUT
  MILK BEVERAGE
2 CARROTS
½ TEASPOON GROUND CARDAMOM
½ TEASPOON GROUND GINGER
1 BLOOD ORANGE, PEELED AND
  SEGMENTED
2 TABLESPOONS WALNUTS
2 TABLESPOONS MASCARPONE OR
  OTHER CREAM CHEESE (OPTIONAL)
2 TABLESPOONS HONEY

Buckwheat and Kamut with Orange, Pomegranate Seeds, and Chocolate

Hold the pomegranate half seed-side down and hit the back with a rolling pin. This should encourage the seeds to drop out more quickly than removing them by hand. Discard the skin and set aside the seeds.

Put the buckwheat into a medium pan, pour in the almond milk, and place over medium heat. Bring to a simmer, cover, and cook for 12 minutes.

Add the kamut flakes and 1½ cups (12 fl oz / 350 ml) water. Cook for another 8 minutes, or until the porridge reaches the desired consistency. Remove from the heat.

Divide the porridge between 2 bowls, top with the orange slices, and sprinkle with the pomegranate seeds and grated chocolate. Drizzle with maple syrup to serve.

SERVES 2
PREPARATION 5 MIN
COOKING 20 MIN

½ POMEGRANATE
½ CUP (2 OZ / 50 G) BUCKWHEAT
1½ CUPS (12 FL OZ / 350 ML)
   ALMOND MILK
½ CUP (2 OZ / 50 G) KAMUT FLAKES
1 ORANGE, PEELED AND SLICED
   INTO ROUNDS
1 OZ (25 G) BITTERSWEET (DARK)
   CHOCOLATE (MINIMUM 70%
   CACAO CONTENT), GRATED
2 TABLESPOONS MAPLE SYRUP

Spelt and Barley with Apricot Compote, Yogurt, and Cashew Nut Butter

Put the apricots into a small pan with 4 tablespoons water and 2 tablespoons of the honey. Place over medium heat and simmer for about 10 minutes, or until the apricots are soft. If the apricots are not soft, add a couple of extra tablespoons of water and continue to cook.

Meanwhile, put the spelt flakes and barley flakes in a medium pan, add the almond milk and 1½ cups (12 fl oz / 350 ml) water and place over high heat. Bring to a boil. Once the liquid has begun to reduce, stir quickly to prevent the porridge from sticking. Cook over medium-high heat for 8–12 minutes, or until the porridge reaches the desired consistency, then remove from the heat.

Divide the porridge between 2 bowls. Top with the cashew butter and apricot compote. Spoon the yogurt over, sprinkle with the flaxseed (linseed) and almond flakes, then drizzle with the remaining honey and any remaining apricot syrup to serve.

SERVES 2
PREPARATION 10 MIN
COOKING 15 MIN

2 VERY RIPE APRICOTS, HALVED
  AND PITTED (STONED),
  OR 4 DRIED APRICOTS
4 TABLESPOONS HONEY
½ CUP (2 OZ / 50 G) SPELT FLAKES
½ CUP (2 OZ / 50 G) BARLEY FLAKES
1½ CUPS (12 FL OZ / 350 ML)
  ALMOND MILK
2 TABLESPOONS CASHEW NUT BUTTER
2–3 TABLESPOONS SKYR YOGURT,
  OR GREEK YOGURT
2 TEASPOONS FLAXSEED (LINSEED)
2 TEASPOONS TOASTED
  FLAKED ALMONDS

Put the strawberries into a bowl and use a fork or potato masher to squash them coarsely. Sprinkle with the stevia or sugar, mix, and allow to macerate for 15 minutes.

Put the rye flakes into a medium pan, pour in the coconut milk beverage and 1½ cups (12 fl oz / 350 ml) water and place over high heat. Bring to a boil. Reduce to medium-high heat and cook for 5 minutes.

Add the oats and cook, stirring, for 5–8 minutes or until the porridge reaches the desired consistency, then remove from the heat.

Divide the porridge between 2 bowls. Spoon the macerated strawberries over the porridge, including any liquid that remains in the bowl. Sprinkle with the chopped cranberries and flaxseed (linseed). Dust with the cinnamon and drizzle with the maple syrup to serve.

Rye and Oats with Smashed Strawberries, Cranberries, and Cinnamon

SERVES 2
PREPARATION 5 MIN, PLUS
15 MIN MACERATING
COOKING 20 MIN

1 CUP (3½ OZ / 100 G) STRAWBERRIES, HULLED
½ TEASPOON STEVIA OR 2 TEASPOONS SUPERFINE (CASTER) SUGAR
½ CUP (2 OZ / 50 G) RYE FLAKES
1½ CUPS (12 FL OZ / 350 ML) COCONUT MILK BEVERAGE
½ CUP (2 OZ / 50 G) ROLLED OATS
2 TEASPOONS DRIED CRANBERRIES, COARSELY CHOPPED
2 TEASPOONS FLAXSEED (LINSEED)
2 TEASPOONS GROUND CINNAMON
2 TABLESPOONS MAPLE SYRUP

4-Grain Porridge with Cherries, Apricots, and Pistachios

Put the barley flakes, wheat flakes, rye flakes, and spelt flakes into a medium pan, pour in the coconut milk and 1½ cups (12 fl oz / 350 ml) water and place over high heat. Bring to a boil. Once the liquid has begun to reduce, stir quickly to prevent the porridge from sticking.

Reduce to medium-high heat and cook for 7–8 minutes, or until the porridge reaches the desired consistency, then remove from the heat.

Meanwhile, put the halved cherries into a small pan and add 2 tablespoons of maple syrup and 2 tablespoons of water. Place over low heat for 3 minutes until the cherries start to soften and the maple syrup is absorbed. The fruit should be soft but still retain some of the shape.

Divide the porridge between 2 bowls. Top with the cherries and apricots, and sprinkle with the pistachios and flaxseed (linseed), if using. Drizzle with the remaining maple syrup to serve.

SERVES 2
PREPARATION 5 MIN
COOKING 10 MIN

¼ CUP (1 OZ / 25 G) BARLEY FLAKES
¼ CUP (1 OZ / 25 G) WHEAT FLAKES
¼ CUP (1 OZ / 25 G) RYE FLAKES
¼ CUP (1 OZ / 25 G) SPELT FLAKES
1½ CUPS (12 FL OZ / 350 ML) COCONUT
  MILK BEVERAGE
½ CUP (2½ OZ / 65 G) CHERRIES,
  HALVED AND PITTED (STONED)
4 TABLESPOONS MAPLE SYRUP
½ CUP (2 OZ / 50 G) DRIED APRICOTS
3 TABLESPOONS SHELLED PISTACHIOS,
  COARSELY CHOPPED
1 TABLESPOON FLAXSEED (LINSEED)
  (OPTIONAL)

Oats and Buckwheat with Sour Cherry, Coconut Yogurt, and Macadamia Nuts

If using dried sour cherries, put them into a small pan, pour in enough water to cover 2 inches (5 cm) and bring to a simmer over medium heat, then remove from the heat and let cool. Let the cherries soak overnight in the refrigerator. Drain and sprinkle with the stevia or sugar.

Alternatively, if using fresh sour cherries, halve them and remove the stones. Sprinkle with the stevia or sugar. Allow to macerate for at least 20 minutes.

Put the oats and buckwheat in a medium pan, add the coconut milk and 1½ cups (12 fl oz / 350 ml) water and place over a medium heat. Bring to a simmer, cover, and cook for 20 minutes, then remove from the heat.

Divide the porridge between 2 bowls. Top with the cherries and coconut yogurt. Sprinkle with the macadamia nuts and drizzle with the maple syrup to serve.

SERVES 2
PREPARATION 5 MIN, PLUS SOAKING OVERNIGHT OR MACERATING
COOKING 20 MIN

½ CUP (2 OZ / 50 G) SOUR CHERRIES, FRESH OR DRIED
½ TEASPOON STEVIA OR 1 TEASPOON SUPERFINE (CASTER) SUGAR
¼ CUP (1½ OZ / 40 G) STEEL-CUT OATS (PINHEAD OATMEAL)
½ CUP (2 OZ / 50 G) BUCKWHEAT
1½ CUPS (12 FL OZ / 350 ML) COCONUT MILK BEVERAGE
2 TABLESPOONS COCONUT YOGURT
2 TABLESPOONS MACADAMIA NUTS, COARSELY CHOPPED
2 TABLESPOONS MAPLE SYRUP

Oats and Barley with Lemon Mousse, Red Currants, and Basil

Whisk the whipping cream until stiff peaks form, then gently fold the lemon curd into the cream. Set aside.

Put the oats and barley flakes into a medium pan, pour in the coconut milk beverage and 1½ cups (12 fl oz / 350 ml) water and bring to a boil. Once the liquid has begun to reduce, stir quickly to prevent the porridge from sticking. Reduce to medium-high heat and cook for 7–8 minutes or until the porridge reaches the desired consistency, then remove from the heat.

Divide the porridge between 2 bowls. Spoon as much of the lemon mousse as you would like onto each bowl of porridge. Top with the red currants and sprinkle with the basil leaves and bee pollen. Drizzle with the honey to serve, if using.

SERVES 2
PREPARATION 5 MIN
COOKING 7 MIN

4 TABLESPOONS (2 FL OZ /
  60 ML) WHIPPING CREAM
¼ CUP (1¼ OZ / 35 G) LEMON CURD
  (SUGAR-FREE IF POSSIBLE)
½ CUP (2 OZ / 50 G) ROLLED OATS
½ CUP (2 OZ / 50 G) BARLEY FLAKES
1½ CUPS (12 FL OZ / 350 ML) COCONUT
  MILK BEVERAGE
⅓ CUP (1¼ OZ / 30 G) RED CURRANTS
2–3 SMALL FRESH BASIL LEAVES,
  FINELY CHOPPED
½ TEASPOON BEE POLLEN (OPTIONAL)
2 TABLESPOONS HONEY (OPTIONAL)

Kamut and Spelt with Passion Fruit, Pink Grapefruit, and Chia Seeds

Put the kamut flakes and spelt flakes into a medium pan, pour in the coconut milk and 1½ cups (12 fl oz / 350 ml) water and place over high heat. Bring to a boil. Once the liquid has begun to reduce, stir quickly to prevent the porridge from sticking.

Reduce to medium-high heat and cook for 7 minutes, or until the porridge reaches the desired consistency, then remove from the heat.

Divide the porridge between 2 bowls. Top with the grapefruit segments and passion fruit pulp, and sprinkle with the chia seeds. Drizzle with the honey to serve.

SERVES 2
PREPARATION 3 MIN
COOKING 7 MIN

½ CUP (2 OZ / 50 G) KAMUT FLAKES
½ CUP (2 OZ / 50 G) SPELT FLAKES
1½ CUPS (12 FL OZ / 350 ML) COCONUT
  MILK BEVERAGE
½ PINK GRAPEFRUIT, PEELED
  SEGMENTED, AND PITH REMOVED
2 PASSION FRUIT, HALVED AND PULP
  SCOOPED OUT
2 TEASPOONS CHIA SEEDS
2 TABLESPOONS HONEY

Millet, Amaranth, and Quinoa with Plums, Nectarines, and Mixed Seeds

Slice the plums or greengages and nectarine in half and remove the pits (stones), then cut in half again lengthwise. Chop the nectarine into cubes. Set aside.

Put the millet, amaranth, and quinoa into a medium pan, pour in the almond milk and 1½ cups (12 fl oz / 350 ml) water and place over medium heat. Bring to a simmer, cover, and cook for 12 minutes. Add the oats and cook for another 8 minutes.

Meanwhile, toast the seeds lightly in a dry skillet (frying pan) over medium heat for 2 minutes. Set aside.

Remove the porridge from the heat and divide between 2 bowls. Top with the nectarine pieces and plum or greengage quarters. Sprinkle with the toasted seeds, dust with the cardamom and drizzle with the honey to serve.

SERVES 2
PREPARATION 5 MIN
COOKING 20 MIN

2 VERY RIPE SMALL PLUMS OR
  GREENGAGES
1 RIPE NECTARINE
3 TABLESPOONS MILLET
3 TABLESPOONS AMARANTH
3 TABLESPOONS QUINOA
1½ CUPS (12 FL OZ / 350 ML)
  ALMOND MILK
¼ CUP (1 OZ / 25 G) ROLLED OATS
2 TABLESPOONS MIX OF SUNFLOWER,
  PUMPKIN, FLAXSEED (LINSEED),
  SESAME, AND CHIA SEEDS
1 TEASPOON GROUND CARDAMOM
2 TABLESPOONS HONEY

If you have a juicing machine, put the carrots through it and reserve both the pulp and the juice. Alternatively, grate the carrots finely, then squeeze the grated carrot to extract the juice. Reserve both the grated carrot and the juice and set aside.

Put the oats, rye flakes, and wheat flakes into a medium pan, pour in the coconut milk beverage and 1¼ cups (10 fl oz / 300 ml) water and bring to a boil. Once the liquid has begun to reduce, stir quickly to prevent the porridge from sticking. Add the reserved carrot juice and cook for 7 minutes, or until the porridge reaches the desired consistency. Remove from the heat.

Divide the porridge between 2 bowls. Top with the grated or pulped carrot and prune pieces, followed by the walnuts and seeds. Drizzle with the maple syrup to serve.

Oats, Rye, and Wheat with Carrots, Walnuts, and Prunes

SERVES 2
PREPARATION 10 MIN
COOKING 7 MIN

2 CARROTS
⅓ CUP (1¼ OZ / 35 G) ROLLED OATS
⅓ CUP (1¼ OZ / 35 G) RYE FLAKES
⅓ CUP (1¼ OZ / 35 G) WHEAT FLAKES
1½ CUPS (12 FL OZ / 350 ML)
  COCONUT MILK BEVERAGE
4 PRUNES, HALVED
¼ CUP (1 OZ / 25 G) WALNUTS
2 TABLESPOONS MIX OF SUNFLOWER
  SEEDS, PUMPKIN SEEDS, AND
  FLAXSEED (LINSEED)
2 TABLESPOONS MAPLE SYRUP

Wheat with Figs, Pecans, Baked Pear, and Vanilla

Preheat the oven to 350°F/180°C/Gas Mark 4. Line a baking sheet with parchment (baking) paper.

Cut the pear in half lengthwise, sprinkle with stevia or sugar and place the halves on the baking sheet. Bake for 20 minutes.

Put the wheat flakes into a medium pan, pour in the almond milk and place over high heat. Bring to a boil. Once the liquid has begun to reduce, stir quickly to prevent the porridge from sticking.

Reduce to medium-high heat and cook for 7–8 minutes, or until the porridge reaches the desired consistency, then remove from the heat.

Stir in the vanilla and divide the porridge between 2 bowls. Top with the fig slices, pecans, and baked pear halves. Drizzle with the honey to serve.

SERVES 2
PREPARATION 2 MIN
COOKING 20 MIN

1 RIPE PEAR
1 TEASPOON STEVIA OR 2 TEASPOONS
  SUPERFINE (CASTER) SUGAR
1 CUP (3½ OZ / 100 G) WHEAT FLAKES
3 CUPS (24 FL OZ / 700 ML)
  ALMOND MILK
2 TEASPOONS VANILLA BEAN PASTE
2 FIGS, THINLY SLICED
½ CUP (2¼ OZ / 60 G) PECANS
2 TABLESPOONS HONEY

Amaranth, Quinoa, and Oats with Almond Butter, Kiwifruit, and Strawberries

Put the amaranth and quinoa into a medium pan, pour in the almond milk and 1½ cups (12 fl oz / 350 ml) water and place over medium heat. Bring to a simmer, cover, and cook for 15 minutes.

Add the oats and reduce the heat to medium-high. You may need to add up to ¼ cup (2 fl oz / 60 ml) more water if most of the liquid has been absorbed. Cook, stirring, for 7–8 minutes, or until the porridge reaches the desired consistency. Remove from the heat.

Divide the porridge between 2 bowls. Top with the almond butter, kiwifruit, and strawberry pieces. Finally, sprinkle over the sesame seeds and drizzle with the honey to serve.

SERVES 2
PREPARATION 5 MIN
COOKING 25 MIN

¼ CUP (2 OZ / 50 G) AMARANTH
3 TABLESPOONS QUINOA
1½ CUPS (12 FL OZ / 350 ML)
  ALMOND MILK
½ CUP (2 OZ / 50 G) REGULAR OATS
2 TABLESPOONS ALMOND BUTTER
2 KIWIFRUIT, PEELED AND DICED
½ CUP (2 OZ / 50 G) STRAWBERRIES,
  HULLED AND QUARTERED
2 TEASPOONS TOASTED SESAME SEEDS
2 TABLESPOONS HONEY

Meat Bowls

Rye and Spelt with Poached Egg, Blood Sausage, and Gruyére

SERVES 2
PREPARATION 5 MIN
COOKING 20–25 MIN

1 TABLESPOON BUTTER
4 SLICES BLOOD SAUSAGE
 (BLACK PUDDING)
1 TABLESPOON OLIVE OIL
1 GARLIC CLOVE, FINELY CHOPPED
1 SHALLOT, FINELY CHOPPED
⅓ CUP (2 OZ / 50 G) RYE FLAKES
⅓ CUP (2 OZ / 50 G) SPELT FLAKES
3¼ CUPS (25 FL OZ / 750 ML)
 CHICKEN BROTH (STOCK)
2 EGGS
2 TABLESPOONS WHITE WINE VINEGAR
4 TABLESPOONS GRATED GRUYÉRE
ARUGULA (ROCKET), TO GARNISH
SALT AND BLACK PEPPER

Place a skillet (frying pan) over medium heat. Add the butter and allow it to bubble before adding the sausage. Cook on both sides for 3 minutes then break it up with a fork. Remove from the heat and set aside in the pan.

Put a medium pan over medium heat. Add the olive oil, garlic, and shallot and cook for 1 minute before adding the rye and spelt flakes. Cook for another 2 minutes before adding the broth (stock). Cook for 7–8 minutes until the grains reach the desired consistency.

Meanwhile, bring a pan of water to a simmer over medium heat, add the vinegar and swirl the water clockwise with a spoon to create a whirlpool. Crack the eggs and drop them, one at a time, into the center of the swirling water but make sure they do not touch each other. The eggs should take 2–3 minutes to cook. The fresher the eggs, the more likely they are to form a perfectly poached egg. Use a slotted spoon to prod an egg white to see if it's firm; if it is then immediately remove the eggs from the water and set aside on a plate lined with paper towels.

Stir the grains quickly until the porridge reaches the desired consistency. Stir in 2 tablespoons of the Gruyère. Season with salt and pepper, then divide the porridge between 2 bowls. Top with the poached egg, sausage, and remaining cheese. Sprinkle with some black pepper and garnish with the arugula (rocket) leaves to serve.

Wheat, Rye, and Barley with Chicken, Squid, and Chorizo

Place a heavy pan over medium heat and add 2 tablespoons of the olive oil. Add the chorizo and chicken thigh pieces. When the chorizo is starting to crisp, add the paprika, oregano, chile, tomato, onion, and garlic. After 2 minutes add the grains. Cook for 3–4 minutes, stirring constantly to prevent burning.

Pour in the fish broth (stock), add the lemon zest, and season to taste with salt. Bring to a boil, then reduce the heat to low. Simmer for 8–10 minutes, or until all the liquid has been absorbed and the grains are soft.

Heat the remaining olive oil in a large skillet (frying pan) over high heat. Fry the squid rings for 2 minutes, until lightly colored. Season with salt and pepper to taste. Remove from the heat.

Divide the grain mixture between 2 plates. Top with the squid rings and sprinkle with the parsley. Serve with a lemon wedge.

SERVES 2
PREPARATION 10 MIN
COOKING 15–20 MIN

4 TABLESPOONS OLIVE OIL
1 OZ / 30 G HIGH-QUALITY CHORIZO,
   SLICED
2 BONELESS CHICKEN
   THIGHS, CHOPPED
1 TEASPOON PAPRIKA
1 TEASPOON DRIED OREGANO
1 SMALL CHILE, FINELY DICED
1 TOMATO, CHOPPED
½ ONION, FINELY CHOPPED
1 GARLIC CLOVES, FINELY CHOPPED
1½ CUPS (5 OZ / 150 G) MIX OF WHEAT,
   RYE, AND BARLEY FLAKES
3 CUPS (26 FL OZ / 720 ML) FISH
   BROTH (STOCK)
1 TEASPOON FINELY GRATED
   LEMON ZEST
⅔ CUP (3½ OZ / 100 G) SQUID RINGS
2 TABLESPOONS CHOPPED PARSLEY
2 LEMON WEDGES
SALT AND BLACK PEPPER

Barley with Slow-Cooked Beef Ragu

Preheat the oven to 275°F/140°C/Gas Mark 1.

Cut the beef into medium-size chunks, put in a bowl, and coat with the flour and a good pinch of salt and pepper. Put 2 tablespoons oil in a skillet (frying pan) and place over high heat. Add the beef and do not move or turn it until a nice crust has formed on each side. Remove the beef from the pan and set aside.

Reduce the heat to medium and add the remaining oil to the same pan. Add the carrot, celery, and garlic and cook for 2 minutes. Pour in the red wine and allow it to reduce a little.

Transfer the contents of the pan into a heavy Dutch oven (casserole dish). Stir in the beef, tomatoes, tomato paste, bay leaves, red wine vinegar, and ½ cup (4 fl oz / 120 ml) beef broth (stock), and season with some more salt and pepper. Cover and place in the oven for a minimum of 4 hours—preferably 5–6 hours. Alternatively, use a slow cooker in place of the Dutch oven.

Once the beef has cooked, put the barley in a medium pan, add 3¼ cups (25 fl oz / 750 ml) beef broth, and place over high heat. Bring to a boil. Once the liquid has begun to reduce, stir quickly to prevent the porridge from sticking.

Reduce to medium-high heat and cook for 7–8 minutes until it reaches the desired consistency, then remove from the heat.

Divide the porridge between 2 bowls. Stir in the oregano before ladling the ragu over the barley. Top with the Parmesan shavings to serve.

SERVES 2
PREPARATION 10 MIN
COOKING 4½–6½ HRS

9 OZ / 250 G CHUCK STEAK
  OR STEWING STEAK
2 TABLESPOONS ALL-PURPOSE (PLAIN)
  FLOUR OR GLUTEN-FREE FLOUR
3 TABLESPOONS VEGETABLE OIL,
  FOR FRYING
1 CARROT, FINELY CHOPPED
1 STALK CELERY, FINELY CHOPPED
2 GARLIC CLOVES, CRUSHED
  AND CHOPPED
1 CUP (8 FL OZ / 250 ML) RED WINE
1 CUP (7 OZ / 200 G) CHOPPED
  CANNED TOMATOES
2 TEASPOONS TOMATO PASTE
2 BAY LEAVES
3¾ CUPS (29 FL OZ / 870 ML)
  BEEF BROTH (STOCK)
2 TABLESPOONS RED WINE VINEGAR
1½ CUPS (5 OZ / 150 G) BARLEY FLAKES
1 TEASPOON DRIED OREGANO
⅓ CUP (1 OZ / 25 G) SHAVED PARMESAN
SALT AND BLACK PEPPER

Buckwheat with Crispy Bacon, Avocado, and Roasted Tomatoes

Place a skillet (frying pan) over medium heat. Add the pancetta or bacon and allow to crisp, then turn over to crisp on the other side. Remove from the heat, set aside on a plate lined with paper towels, then snip into small pieces.

Preheat the oven to 350°F/180°C/Gas Mark 4.

Put the tomatoes into a baking dish, add the extra virgin olive oil, and turn to coat them. Sprinkle with the oregano and some salt and pepper. Bake in the oven for 45 minutes, or until just black at the edges. Remove from the oven. Reserve a few tomatoes for the garnish and put the rest into a blender and blend to a puree.

Place a medium pan over medium heat. Add 1 tablespoon of the olive oil, the onion and garlic, and cook for 2–3 minutes, or until translucent. Add the buckwheat and pour in the red wine. Allow the wine to be absorbed by the buckwheat, then add the tomato puree. Cook for 20 minutes, or until the puree has almost all been absorbed. Remove from the heat.

Stir in the Parmesan and divide the buckwheat between 2 plates. Top with the avocado, pancetta or bacon, and reserved tomatoes. Sprinkle with a little salt and pepper to serve.

SERVES 2
PREPARATION 10 MIN
COOKING 1¼ HRS

4 SLICES (RASHERS) PANCETTA OR
   LEAN (STREAKY) BACON
1 LB / 450 G CHERRY TOMATOES
4 TABLESPOONS EXTRA VIRGIN
   OLIVE OIL
2 TEASPOONS DRIED OREGANO
2 TABLESPOONS OLIVE OIL
1 ONION, FINELY CHOPPED
2 GARLIC CLOVES, FINELY CHOPPED
1 CUP (6 OZ / 175 G) BUCKWHEAT
¼ CUP (2 FL OZ / 60 ML) RED WINE
2 TEASPOONS GRATED PARMESAN
½ AVOCADO, SLICED
SALT AND BLACK PEPPER

Farro with Crispy Pork, Cauliflower, and Raisin Puree

SERVES 2
PREPARATION 10 MIN
COOKING 30 MIN

2 PORK SCALLOPS (ESCALOPES)
2 TABLESPOONS ALL-PURPOSE (PLAIN)
  FLOUR, FOR DUSTING
⅔ CUP (5 FL OZ / 150 ML) HEAVY
  (DOUBLE) CREAM
⅔ CUP (5 FL OZ / 150 ML) MILK
1½ CUPS (5 OZ / 150 G)
  CAULIFLOWER FLORETS
PINCH SEA SALT
2 TABLESPOONS RAISINS
¼ CUP (2 FL OZ / 60 ML) WHITE WINE
2 TEASPOONS BROWN SUGAR
1 TEASPOON UNSALTED BUTTER
2 TABLESPOONS FINELY
  CHOPPED SHALLOTS
¾ CUP (5 OZ / 150 G) PEARLED
  ITALIAN FARRO (PEARLED SPELT)
2 CUPS (16 FL OZ / 475 ML)
  VEGETABLE BROTH (STOCK)
1 TEASPOON FINELY CHOPPED THYME
1 TABLESPOON GRATED PARMESAN
2 TABLESPOONS OLIVE OIL
SALT AND PEPPER
FRESH PEA SHOOTS, TO GARNISH

Put the pork scallops (escalopes) between two sheets of plastic wrap (clingfilm) and flatten them with a rolling pin to a thin layer. Remove the plastic wrap and slice each piece of pork into thin strips. Dust with the flour and season with salt and pepper, then set aside.

Pour the cream and milk into a medium pan over medium heat and bring to a boil. Add the cauliflower florets along with a big pinch of sea salt. Simmer for 5 minutes or until the cauliflower is soft. Strain the cauliflower. Transfer all but 2 florets to a food processor and process to a puree. Scrape into a bowl and clean the food processor.

Put the raisins, white wine, and brown sugar into a small pan, place over medium heat, and simmer for 5 minutes. Remove from the heat, allow to cool a little, then transfer to the cleaned food processor and blend to a puree.

Heat the butter in a pan over medium heat and fry the shallots until softened. Add the farro (pearled spelt) and stir to coat in the butter and shallots. Add the broth (stock) and thyme and cook for 20 minutes. Once almost all the liquid has been absorbed, add the cauliflower puree and continue to cook until the farro is soft. Add the Parmesan and season to taste.

Place a skillet (frying pan) over high heat, add the olive oil and fry the pork for 1–2 minutes on each side until crispy.

Divide the farro between 2 bowls. Top with the pork slices and a spoonful of the raisin puree. Garnish with pea shoots to serve.

Rye and Buckwheat with Salami, Porcini, and Parmesan

Put the porcini mushrooms into a bowl and pour in 1 cup (8 fl oz / 250 ml) boiling water, or enough to cover. Let soak for 15 minutes. Strain the porcini, reserving the liquid, then coarsely chop.

Put the oil and butter in a large heavy pan, place over medium heat, and add the salami, onion, garlic, rosemary, thyme, and porcini. Cook for 1–2 minutes and season to taste with salt and pepper. Add the buckwheat, stirring constantly, pour in the red wine, and cook for 10 minutes, or until the liquid has almost completely been absorbed.

Stir in 1 cup (8 fl oz / 250 ml) of the reserved porcini mushroom liquid, then pour in the chicken broth (stock) and cook for 10 minutes, or until the liquid has been almost completely absorbed. Add the rye flakes and cook for another 10 minutes. Taste, and add more seasoning if needed. Remove from the heat.

Remove the thyme sprigs and divide between 2 bowls. Sprinkle with the Parmesan to serve.

SERVES 2
PREPARATION 10 MIN,
PLUS 15 MIN SOAKING
COOKING 35 MIN

1 CUP (¾ OZ / 20 G) DRY
   PORCINI MUSHROOMS
1 TABLESPOON OLIVE OIL
1 TABLESPOON UNSALTED BUTTER
2 OZ / 50 G SALAMI, SLICED
½ ONION, FINELY CHOPPED
1 GARLIC CLOVE, FINELY CHOPPED
2 SPRIGS ROSEMARY, NEEDLES REMOVED
   AND CHOPPED
2 SPRIGS THYME
½ CUP (3 OZ / 85 G) BUCKWHEAT
1 CUP (8 FL OZ / 250 ML) RED WINE
1 CUP (8 FL OZ / 250 ML) CHICKEN
   BROTH (STOCK)
½ CUP (2 OZ / 50 G) RYE FLAKES
1 TABLESPOON GRATED PARMESAN
SALT AND BLACK PEPPER

Place the ham in a sealable container and pour in just enough water to cover. Soak the ham overnight, changing the water twice.

Prcheat the oven to 350°F/180°C/Gas Mark 4.

Drain the ham and put into a large roasting pan. Cover tightly with aluminum foil and bake for 3 hours. Remove the ham from the oven and increase the heat to 400°F/200°C/Gas Mark 6. Mix the mustard, honey, brown sugar, cloves, and rosemary together and rub the mixture all over the ham. Return to the oven and bake for another 30 minutes.

During the ham's final 30 minutes, place a medium pan over medium heat. Add 1 tablespoon of the oil, all the butter, and the onion. Let the onion sweat for 1–2 minutcs. Add the farro (pearled spelt) and the white wine. Pour in the broth (stock) and cook, stirring occasionally as the liquid is absorbed, for 30–40 minutes, or until the farro is tender. Add more broth if required.

Place a small skillet (frying pan) over medium heat, add the remaining olive oil, and fry the sausage slices for 3 minutes on each side, then break up with a fork.

To serve, divide the farro between 2 bowls and top with slices of the ham, the crumbled sausage, and onion jam.

Farro with Roast Ham, Blood Sausage, and Onion Jam

SERVES 2
PREPARATION 10 MIN, PLUS SOAKING OVERNIGHT
COOKING 3¾ HRS

1 LB 2 OZ / 500 G UNCOOKED SMOKED HAM JOINT (WITH A LAYER OF FAT)
3 TABLESPOONS ENGLISH MUSTARD
2 TEASPOONS HONEY
3 TABLESPOONS BROWN SUGAR
½ TEASPOON GROUND CLOVES
1 TEASPOON CHOPPED ROSEMARY NEEDLES
2 TABLESPOONS OLIVE OIL
2 TEASPOONS BUTTER
4 TABLESPOONS SLICED ONION
¾ CUP (5 OZ / 150 G) PEARLED ITALIAN FARRO (PEARLED SPELT)
SPLASH OF DRY WHITE WINE
2½ CUPS (20 FL OZ / 600 ML) CHICKEN BROTH (STOCK)
4 SLICES BLOOD SAUSAGE (BLACK PUDDING)
2 TABLESPOONS ONION JAM

Barley with Veal Meatballs, Zucchini, and Porcini Cream

Put the porcini mushrooms into a heatproof bowl. Pour a little boiling water over them and allow to rehydrate for 15 minutes. Strain the porcini, reserving the liquid, then coarsely chop.

Mix the veal with the mashed potato, dill, and egg and season with salt and pepper. Using your hands, form into small walnut-size meatballs.

Place a medium pan over medium heat. Add the butter and let it foam before adding the meatballs, shallot, and garlic. Cook for 3 minutes, then add the diced zucchini (courgette) and cook for another 2 minutes. Add the chopped porcini and the cream, and simmer for 5–10 minutes. Set aside.

Place a large pan over medium heat, add the barley flakes and pour in the beef broth (stock). Cook for 7–8 minutes, or until the liquid has been absorbed.

To serve, spoon the barley onto 2 plates and sprinkle with the Parmesan. Spoon the meatballs and sauce next to the barley and sprinkle with the parsley.

SERVES 2
PREPARATION 10 MIN,
PLUS 15 MIN SOAKING
COOKING 20–25 MIN

1¾ CUPS (1½ OZ / 35 G) DRY PORCINI
  MUSHROOMS
11 OZ / 300 G GROUND (MINCED) VEAL
¼ CUP (3 OZ / 80 G) MASHED POTATO
2 TEASPOONS FINELY CHOPPED DILL
1 EGG
2 TABLESPOONS UNSALTED BUTTER
½ SHALLOT, FINELY CHOPPED
½ GARLIC CLOVE, FINELY CHOPPED
½ ZUCCHINI (COURGETTE), DICED
¼ CUP (2 FL OZ / 60 ML) HEAVY
  (DOUBLE) CREAM
1½ CUPS (5 OZ / 150 G) FLAKED BARLEY
3 CUPS (24 FL OZ / 720 ML) BEEF
  BROTH (STOCK)
2 TABLESPOONS GRATED PARMESAN
2 TEASPOONS FINELY CHOPPED PARSLEY
SALT AND BLACK PEPPER

Oats, Rye, and Spelt Spanish Breakfast Porridge

Set a skillet (frying pan) over medium-high heat, add the chorizo, and cook for 4–5 minutes, stirring frequently. After 3 minutes, add the tomatoes.

At the same time, add the grains and broth (stock) to a large pan, and place over high heat. Bring to a boil. Reduce the heat to medium-high and cook for 7–8 minutes, or until the porridge reaches the desired consistency. Remove from the heat.

Meanwhile, bring a pan of water to a simmer over medium heat, add the vinegar and swirl the water clockwise with a spoon to create a whirlpool. Crack the eggs and drop them, one at a time, into the center of the swirling water but make sure they do not touch each other. The eggs should take 2–3 minutes to cook. The fresher the eggs, the more likely they are to form a perfectly poached egg. Use a slotted spoon to prod an egg white to see if it's firm; if it is then immediately remove the eggs from the water and set aside on a plate lined with paper towels.

Once the chorizo is browned and the tomatoes are warmed through, remove from the heat and stir in the oregano.

Divide the porridge between 2 bowls, top with the chorizo and tomato mixture and a poached egg. Drizzle with the maple syrup and season with salt and pepper to serve.

SERVES 2
PREPARATION 10 MIN
COOKING 10–15 MIN

3½ OZ (100 G) HIGH-QUALITY CHORIZO
  SAUSAGE, FINELY CHOPPED
10–15 CHERRY TOMATOES, QUARTERED
⅓ CUP (1¼ OZ / 35 G) ROLLED OATS
⅓ CUP (1¼ OZ / 35 G) RYE
⅓ CUP (1¼ OZ / 35 G) SPELT FLAKES
3 CUPS (24 FL OZ / 720 ML)
  CHICKEN BROTH (STOCK)
2 TABLESPOONS WHITE WINE VINEGAR
2 EGGS
½ TEASPOON DRIED OREGANO
4 TABLESPOONS MAPLE SYRUP
SALT AND BLACK PEPPER

Black Rice Chicken Congee

SERVES 2
PREPARATION 5 MIN
COOKING 50 MIN

2 GARLIC CLOVES, PEELED

2 TABLESPOONS COARSELY CHOPPED
  FRESH GINGER

1 TEASPOON OLIVE OIL, PLUS
  EXTRA FOR FRYING

2½ CUPS (20 FL OZ / 600 ML)
  CHICKEN BROTH (STOCK)

½ CUP (3½ OZ / 100 G) BLACK RICE

2 LARGE BONELESS CHICKEN THIGHS

ALL-PURPOSE (PLAIN) FLOUR,
  FOR DUSTING

2 TABLESPOONS SALTED PEANUTS OR
  CASHEWS, COARSELY CHOPPED

2 TABLESPOONS LIGHT SOY SAUCE

2 SCALLIONS (SPRING ONIONS),
  COARSELY CHOPPED

SALT AND BLACK PEPPER

Put the garlic, ginger, and olive oil, into a mortar and use a pestle (or a small food processor) to grind them until you have a paste.

Put 2 cups (16 fl oz / 475 ml) of the broth (stock) into a medium pan and bring to a simmer. Add the black rice and allow to simmer, covered, over low heat for 30 minutes, or until almost all the broth has been absorbed. Remove from the heat, cover, and set aside.

Sprinkle the chicken with a little flour. Heat a small skillet (frying pan) over high heat, add a little olive oil, then the chicken thighs. Do not move the thighs or shake the pan; this allows caramelization to take place.

Turn the thighs after a couple of minutes. Reduce the heat a little and cook for another few minutes. Once cooked all the way through, remove the chicken thighs from the heat and shred the meat on a clean cutting board.

Add the remaining ½ cup (4 fl oz / 120 ml) broth to the black rice, along with the garlic-ginger paste, and stir over low heat for 10 minutes.

Divide the rice between 2 bowls and top with the chicken, nuts, soy sauce, and scallions (spring onions). Season with salt and pepper to taste, and serve.

Barley and Spelt with Braised Pork Cheeks, Apple, and Parmesan

SERVES 2
PREPARATION 20 MIN
COOKING 2–3 HRS FOR THE PORK,
8–12 MIN FOR THE GRAINS

11 OZ / 300 G PORK CHEEKS OR PORK
  SHOULDER OR BELLY
2 TABLESPOONS OLIVE OIL
1 ONION, FINELY CHOPPED
1 CARROT, FINELY CHOPPED
2 GARLIC CLOVES, FINELY CHOPPED
2 TEASPOONS HONEY
2 TABLESPOONS RED WINE VINEGAR
1 TEASPOON CHINESE FIVE-SPICE BLEND
5 CUPS (40 FL OZ / 1.2 LITERS)
  CHICKEN BROTH (STOCK)
1 TABLESPOON BUTTER
1 SMALL GALA APPLE, DICED
1½ CUPS (5 OZ / 150 G) MIX OF BARLEY
  AND ROLLED SPELT FLAKES
2 TABLESPOONS GRATED PARMESAN
SALT AND BLACK PEPPER

Trim the pork cheeks of any sinew and season with salt and pepper. Place a medium heavy pan over medium-high heat, add 1 tablespoon of olive oil, and fry the pork for 3–4 minutes on each side until golden brown. Avoid moving the pork too often in the pan. Remove from the pan and set aside.

Reduce the heat to medium and, in the same pan, add the remaining oil, and the onion, carrot, and garlic and cook for 5 minutes, or until softened. Add the honey and cook for 2 minutes, then add the red wine vinegar, Chinese five-spice, and 4¼ cups (34 fl oz / 1 liter) of the stock. Add the pork, cover the pan, and reduce the heat. Simmer for 2–3 hours.

Preheat the oven to 225°F/110°C/Gas Mark ¼. Remove the pork from the broth (stock) and pull the meat from the fat, then set aside in the oven to keep warm.

Put the butter and diced apple into another pan and place over medium heat. Allow the apple to caramelize for 2–3 minutes, then add the barley and spelt flakes and season to taste. Ladle in the broth and vegetables from the pork pan, and pour in more chicken broth if needed. You will need about 4¼ cups (34 fl oz / 1 liter) broth. When almost all the broth has been absorbed, stir in half the grated Parmesan.

Divide the barley and spelt between 2 plates. Top with the pork and sprinkle with the remaining Parmesan.

Using a mandoline, food processor, or sharp knife, slice the kohlrabi into thin matchsticks. Put the sticks into a sealable container, such as a clean jam jar. Set aside.

Put the vinegar, water, honey, salt, ginger, garlic, chili flakes, and peppercorns, into a medium pan over a high heat and bring to a boil. Once the brine is boiling vigorously, remove it from the heat and carefully pour it over the kohlrabi. Let cool, then cover and refrigerate.

Preheat the oven to 275°F/140°C/Gas Mark 1.

Mix the cumin, ground coriander, smoked paprika, garlic powder, brown sugar, sea salt, and some pepper in a bowl. Sprinkle the mixture over the pork and rub into the meat.

Place the pork on a deep baking sheet and pour in 1 cup (1 cup / 250 ml) chicken broth (stock). Cover the pork with aluminum foil and roast in the oven for 6–8 hours, or until extremely tender.

When the pork is ready, put a medium pan over high heat and add the pearl barley and remaining 2½ cups (18 fl oz / 550 ml) broth. Bring to a boil, then reduce the heat and simmer until the broth has reduced by half. Add the red onion chutney. When the liquid is nearly evaporated, stir in the cheddar cheese.

When you are ready to serve, stir the cider vinegar into the barley and divide between 2 plates. Pull apart the pork and arrange it over the top of the barley, along with as much of the pickled kohlrabi as you like.

Make a simple vinaigrette for the salad by whisking the olive oil, lemon juice, and salt and pepper to taste. Toss the salad leaves with the vinaigrette and serve with the barley and pork.

Pearl Barley with Slow-Roasted Pork, Pickled Kohlrabi, and Micro Salad

SERVES 2
PREPARATION 15 MIN,
PLUS CHILLING
COOKING 6 HRS

FOR THE PICKLED KOHLRABI
3½ OZ / 100 G KOHLRABI
   (BULB ONLY), CLEANED AND TRIMMED
4 TABLESPOONS RED WINE VINEGAR
4 TABLESPOONS WATER
1 TEASPOON HONEY
1 TEASPOON SEA SALT
½ TEASPOON GRATED FRESH GINGER
½ GARLIC CLOVE, GRATED
PINCH OF CHILI FLAKES
¼ TEASPOON BLACK PEPPERCORNS

FOR THE PORK
½ TEASPOON GROUND CUMIN
½ TEASPOON GROUND CORIANDER
2 TEASPOONS SMOKED PAPRIKA
2 TEASPOONS GARLIC POWDER
2 TABLESPOONS BROWN SUGAR
2 TEASPOONS SEA SALT
PINCH BLACK PEPPER
14 OZ / 400 G BONELESS PORK
   (SHOULDER, LEG, OR NECK)
3½ CUPS (28 FL OZ / 850 ML)
   CHICKEN BROTH (STOCK)
¾ CUP (5 OZ / 150 G) PEARL BARLEY
2 TEASPOONS RED ONION CHUTNEY
2 TABLESPOONS GRATED
   CHEDDAR CHEESE
2 TEASPOONS APPLE CIDER VINEGAR

TO SERVE
1–2 TABLESPOONS OLIVE OIL
1–2 TABLESPOONS LEMON JUICE
MICROGREEN SALAD

Quinoa and Buckwheat with Chorizo, Tomato, and Watercress

SERVES 2
PREPARATION 10 MIN
COOKING 2½ HRS

1 TABLESPOON OLIVE OIL

1 ONION, FINELY CHOPPED

2 GARLIC CLOVES, FINELY CHOPPED

2 OZ / 50 G HIGH-QUALITY CHORIZO
 SAUSAGE, SLICED

¼ CUP (2 FL OZ / 60 ML) RED WINE

1 CUP (7 OZ / 200 G) CHOPPED
 FRESH TOMATOES

½ RED ONION, SLICED

⅔ CUP (3½ OZ / 100 G) CANNED
 LIMA (BUTTER) BEANS

1 BOUQUET GARNI

¼ CUP (1½ OZ / 40 G) BUCKWHEAT

3 TABLESPOONS QUINOA

3 CUPS (24 FL OZ / 720 ML)
 CHICKEN BROTH (STOCK)

1 CUP (¾ OZ / 20 G) WATERCRESS,
 COARSELY CHOPPED, PLUS
 2 SPRIGS TO GARNISH

SALT AND BLACK PEPPER

Preheat the oven to 325°F/160°C/Gas Mark 3.

Heat the olive oil in a large pan over medium heat, add the onion and garlic, and cook for 2–3 minutes, or until softened. Add the chorizo and allow it to crisp a little before pouring in the red wine. Cook for 4–5 minutes.

Transfer the chorizo mixture to a heavy Dutch oven (casserole dish) along with the chopped tomatoes, red onion, lima beans, 2 tablespoons water, and the bouquet garni. Cook in the oven for 2 hours. Alternatively, use a slow cooker, following the same procedure, and cook on high for 2 hours.

Once cooked, season with salt and pepper and remove the bouquet garni.

Put the buckwheat and quinoa into a medium pan, pour in the chicken broth (stock), and place over a high heat. Bring to a boil, then reduce the heat to low and simmer for 15 minutes, stirring occasionally.

Stir the chopped watercress into the chorizo mixture. Divide the grains between 2 bowls, top with the chorizo mixture and garnish with the sprigs of watercress to serve.

Farro with Braised Lamb, Asparagus, and Garlic Cream

SERVES 2
PREPARATION 10 MIN
COOKING 2¼ HRS, PLUS RESTING

FOR THE LAMB
2 TABLESPOONS OLIVE OIL
9 OZ / 250 G LAMB NECK
½ ONION, FINELY DICED
1 GARLIC CLOVE, FINELY DICED
1 CELERY STALK, CHOPPED
1 SMALL CARROT, CHOPPED
½ SMALL LEEK, WHITE
   PART FINELY SLICED
2 TEASPOONS CHOPPED THYME
2 TEASPOONS ROSEMARY NEEDLES
2 BAY LEAVES
¼ CUP (2 FL OZ / 60 ML)
   DRY WHITE WINE
¾ CUP (6 FL OZ / 175 ML)
   CHICKEN BROTH (STOCK)

FOR THE GARLIC CREAM
1 TABLESPOON VEGETABLE OIL
3 GARLIC CLOVES, IN THEIR SKINS
2 TABLESPOONS WHITE WINE
¼ CUP (2 FL OZ / 60 ML) HEAVY
   (DOUBLE) CREAM
1 TEASPOON DIJON MUSTARD

FOR THE PORRIDGE
2 TABLESPOONS OLIVE OIL
4 TABLESPOONS SLICED ONION
¾ CUP (5 OZ / 150 G) PEARLED ITALIAN
   FARRO (PEARLED SPELT)
SPLASH OF DRY WHITE WINE
2½ CUPS (20 FL OZ / 600 ML)
   VEGETABLE BROTH (STOCK)
2 OZ / 50 G ASPARAGUS
4 TABLESPOONS GRATED PARMESAN

Put a medium pan over high heat, add the olive oil and fry the lamb for 3–4 minutes until crispy on all sides.

Remove the lamb from the pan and set aside. Add the onion, garlic, celery, carrot, leek, and herbs to the pan. Cook over medium heat for 5 minutes, then pour in the white wine, stir, and pour in the chicken broth (stock). Bring to a simmer and return the lamb to the pan. Cover and simmer very gently for 2 hours. Let rest for a while before serving.

Meanwhile, make the garlic cream. Place a small pan over a low heat, add the vegetable oil and the garlic cloves in their skins. Cover and cook for 3 minutes. Gently shake the pan, then cook for 2–3 minutes. Remove the garlic from the pan. Pour in the wine, increase the heat to medium, and add the cream. Pop the garlic cloves out of their skins and into the cream, simmer for 3 minutes, then remove from the heat. Stir in the mustard, transfer to a small food processor, and process until smooth. Set aside.

Place a pan over medium heat and add 1 tablespoon of the oil and the sliced onion. Sweat the onion for 1–2 minutes. Add the farro (pearled spelt) and a splash of white wine. Pour in enough vegetable broth (stock) to cover and cook for 30–40 minutes, stirring occasionally, until the liquid is absorbed. If the farro is not tender, continue to cook and add more broth if required.

Chop the asparagus into slices but keep the tips whole. Add the chopped asparagus to the farro when almost all the broth has been absorbed. Cook for 5 minutes, then add half the Parmesan.

Meanwhile, fill a small pan with water, place over high heat and bring to a boil. Add the asparagus tips and blanch for 2 minutes. Remove with a slotted spoon and set aside.

Divide the farro between 2 bowls. Shred the lamb a little before adding it to the bowls and top with the asparagus tips and a spoonful of the garlic cream. Sprinkle with the remaining Parmesan to serve.

Farro with Spring Lamb, Morels, and Hazelnuts

SERVES 2
PREPARATION 15 MINS
COOKING 40 MINS

2 TEASPOONS UNSALTED BUTTER

2 TABLESPOONS FINELY CHOPPED
SHALLOTS

¾ CUP (5 OZ/150 G) PEARLED ITALIAN
FARRO (PEARLED SPELT)

2½ CUPS (20 FL OZ / 600 ML)
VEGETABLE BROTH (STOCK)

1 TEASPOON FINELY CHOPPED
FRESH THYME

3 TABLESPOONS OLIVE OIL

8 FRESH MOREL MUSHROOMS

½–1 GARLIC CLOVE, FINELY DICED

2 TEASPOONS FINELY DICED SHALLOT

2 TEASPOONS WHITE WINE

⅓ CUP (2½ FL OZ / 80 ML)
CHICKEN BROTH (STOCK)

4 LAMB RIB CHOPS (LAMB CUTLETS)

1 TEASPOON FINELY CHOPPED FRESH
CHERVIL OR ½ TEASPOON DRIED

2 TEASPOONS MASCARPONE

1 TABLESPOON GRATED PARMESAN

2 TABLESPOONS COLD BUTTER, DICED

2 TABLESPOONS COARSELY CHOPPED
HAZELNUTS

SALT AND BLACK PEPPER

Heat the butter over medium heat in a skillet (frying pan) and fry the shallots until softened. Add the pearled farro (pearled spelt) and stir to coat. Pour in 2 cups (16 fl oz / 475 ml) vegetable broth (stock), then the thyme. Cover and simmer for 30–40 minutes, stirring occasionally, until the farro is soft. Add the remaining broth if the farro has absorbed too much liquid. Remove from the heat.

Meanwhile, put a medium pan over medium heat, add 2 tablespoons olive oil and fry the morels, garlic, and diced shallot until golden brown. Add the white wine, cover, and let the wine evaporate for 30–60 seconds, then add the chicken broth. Cover and cook for 6–8 minutes until the broth has evaporated. Remove from the heat and reserve the mushrooms for later.

Before the farro has completely finished cooking, place a skillet (frying pan) over medium-high heat and add 1 tablespoon olive oil. Season the lamb with salt and pepper, add it to the pan, and cook for 1–2 minutes on each side (it should be rare).

To finish, stir the chervil, mascarpone, Parmesan, and diced butter into the farro and divide between 2 plates. Top with the morels and the lamb and sprinkle over the hazelnuts to serve.

To make the parsley cream, combine the wine, garlic, and shallots in a small heavy pan. Simmer over medium heat for 3–4 minutes, or until the mixture is reduced by a third. Stir in the whipping cream and parsley, then simmer for 2–3 minutes, or until the mixture is reduced by about a third again, to about 4 tablespoons. Transfer the mixture to a blender or mini processor, and blend until the parsley is finely chopped.

Preheat the oven to 350°F/180°C/Gas Mark 4. Season the rabbit legs with salt and pepper, then wrap with the pancetta or bacon. Put the rabbit legs into a small baking dish and pour in the ¼ cup (2 fl oz / 60 ml) broth (stock). Bake for 35–40 minutes, then remove from the oven and allow to rest for 5 minutes.

Meanwhile, make the porridge. Heat the butter in a medium pan over medium heat. Once bubbling, add the garlic, mushrooms, celery, onion, and thyme leaves. Cook for 2 minutes, then pour in the wine. Cook for 3 minutes, add the broth, and season with salt and pepper. Add the pearl barley, cover, and cook over low heat for 20 minutes.

Add the celery root (celeriac) and cook for another 20 minutes, or until the pearl barley and the celery root are tender and the broth has been absorbed. Season to taste.

Divide the barley mixture between 2 plates. Top with the rabbit legs and the parsley cream.

Pearl Barley with Roast Rabbit, Celery Root, and Parsley Cream

SERVES 2
PREPARATION 15 MIN
COOKING 45 MIN

2 RABBIT LEGS
4 SLICES (RASHERS) PANCETTA
  OR LEAN (STREAKY) BACON
¼ CUP (2 FL OZ / 60 ML)
  CHICKEN BROTH (STOCK)
SALT AND BLACK PEPPER

FOR THE PORRIDGE
1 TABLESPOON BUTTER
2 GARLIC CLOVES, CHOPPED
1 OZ / 25 G BUTTON
  MUSHROOMS, SLICED
¼ STALK CELERY, FINELY CHOPPED
¼ ONION, FINELY CHOPPED
LEAVES FROM 1 SPRIG THYME
1½ CUPS (12 FL OZ / 350 ML)
  WHITE WINE
1½ CUPS (12 FL OZ / 350 ML)
  CHICKEN BROTH (STOCK)
¾ CUP (5 OZ / 150 G) PEARL BARLEY
¼ CUP (1½ OZ / 40 G) CELERY ROOT
  (CELERIAC), CUT INTO ½ INCH
  (1 CM) DICE

FOR THE PARSLEY CREAM
3 TABLESPOONS DRY WHITE WINE
½ LARGE GARLIC CLOVE,
  FINELY CHOPPED
½ LARGE SHALLOT, FINELY CHOPPED
3 TABLESPOONS WHIPPING CREAM
2 TABLESPOONS CHOPPED PARSLEY

Oats, Rye, and Wheat with Poached Eggs, Crispy Bacon, and Maple Syrup

Half fill a medium pan with water and place over high heat. Bring to a boil, then reduce to a simmer.

Add the grains and broth (stock) to a large pan, then place over high heat. Bring to a boil. Reduce to medium-high heat and cook for 7–8 minutes, or until the porridge reaches the desired consistency. Remove from the heat.

Meanwhile, once the porridge has been cooking for 4 minutes, add the vinegar to the pan of simmering water and swirl the water clockwise with a spoon to create a whirlpool. Crack the eggs and drop them, one at a time, into the center of the swirling water but make sure they do not touch each other. The eggs should take 2–3 minutes to cook. The fresher the eggs, the more likely they are to form a perfectly poached egg. Use a slotted spoon to prod an egg white to see if it's firm; if it is then immediately remove the eggs from the water and set aside on a plate lined with paper towels.

Set a skillet (frying pan) over medium-high heat and add the bacon slices (rashers). Once crisp on both sides, remove from the heat and place the bacon on a plate lined with paper towels.

Divide the porridge between 2 bowls. Top with the eggs and crispy bacon slices. Drizzle with the maple syrup and season with salt and pepper to serve.

SERVES 2
PREPARATION 5 MIN
COOKING 10 MIN

⅓ CUP (1¼ OZ / 35 G) ROLLED OATS
⅓ CUP (1¼ OZ / 35 G) RYE FLAKES
⅓ CUP (1¼ OZ / 35 G) WHEAT FLAKES
3 CUPS (24 FL OZ / 720 ML)
  CHICKEN BROTH (STOCK)
2 TABLESPOONS WHITE WINE VINEGAR
4 EGGS
6 SLICES (RASHERS) LEAN
  (STREAKY) BACON
6 TABLESPOONS MAPLE SYRUP
SALT AND PEPPER

Farro with Goat Curd, Fava Beans, and Pancetta

Put 1 tablespoon oil, 1 teaspoon butter, and the onion in a medium pan over medium heat. Let the onion sweat for 1–2 minutes, then add the farro (pearled spelt) and white wine. Pour in the broth (stock) to cover the farro. Cook for 40 minutes, or until the farro is tender and soft, stirring frequently as the liquid is absorbed. You can add more broth if the farro has absorbed too much liquid.

Meanwhile, place a small pan over medium heat and add the remaining oil and butter. Once bubbling, add the leek and cook for 8 minutes, or until just tender.

Bring a pan of salted water to a boil and blanch the fava (broad) beans for 2–3 minutes, then drain and set aside.

Place a skillet (frying pan) over high heat and cook the pancetta on both sides until crispy.

Once the farro is ready, stir in the leeks and half the fava beans and season to taste. Divide the farro between 2 bowls. Top with the goat curd or soft goat cheese and the remaining fava beans. Crumble over the pancetta to serve.

SERVES 2
PREPARATION 5 MIN
COOKING 40 MIN

4 TABLESPOONS OLIVE OIL
2 TEASPOONS BUTTER
4 TABLESPOONS SLICED ONION
¾ CUP (5 OZ / 150 G) PEARLED
  ITALIAN FARRO (PEARLED SPELT)
2 TABLESPOONS DRY WHITE WINE
2½ CUPS (20 FL OZ / 600 ML)
  VEGETABLE BROTH (STOCK)
1 LEEK, WHITE PART ONLY, SLICED
  INTO FINE DISKS
½ CUP (3OZ / 80 G) FAVA
  (BROAD) BEANS
4 TABLESPOONS GOAT CURD OR
  SOFT GOAT CHEESE
2 SLICES (RASHERS) PANCETTA
SALT AND PEPPER

Pearl Barley with Vodka Duck, Star Anise, and Lemon Thyme

SERVES 2
PREPARATION 10 MIN,
PLUS 12 HOURS MARINATING
COOKING 1¼ HRS

½ CUP (4 FL OZ / 120 ML) VODKA
2 STAR ANISE
4 WHOLE CLOVES
1 TEASPOON FRESHLY GROUND
  BLACK PEPPER
½ TEASPOON SALT
2 DUCK LEGS
2 SMALL CARROTS
2 TABLESPOONS APPLE CIDER VINEGAR
1 TEASPOON LEMON THYME LEAVES,
  PLUS EXTRA TO SPRINKLE
2½ CUPS (20 FL OZ / 600 ML)
  CHICKEN BROTH (STOCK)
¾ CUP (5 OZ / 150 G) PEARL BARLEY
4 TABLESPOONS WHIPPING CREAM
2 TABLESPOONS GRATED PARMESAN

Combine the vodka, star anise, cloves, pepper, and salt in a bowl. Add the duck legs and coat in the mixture. Cover the bowl with plastic wrap (clingfilm) and refrigerate for a minimum of 12 hours, turning the legs after 6 hours.

Peel the carrots, then use the peeler to peel into long, thin strands. Put the strands into a bowl, add the cider vinegar and lemon thyme, and season to taste with salt and pepper. Refrigerate until needed.

Preheat the oven to 350°F/180°C/Gas Mark 4.

Put the duck legs into a baking dish, season with a little salt, and roast in the oven for 1 hour. Turn off the oven and allow the meat to rest with the oven door open for 10 minutes.

When the duck legs have been roasting for 30 minutes pour 2 cups (16 fl oz / 475 ml) chicken broth (stock) into a medium pan and bring to a simmer over medium heat. Add the pearl barley and simmer over medium-low heat for 30 minutes.

Once almost all the broth has been absorbed, add the cream and the remaining stock. Cook for 10–15 minutes until this has almost all been absorbed, then stir in the grated Parmesan.

Divide the pearl barley between 2 plates. Add a duck leg to each plate and top with the carrot strands. Sprinkle with lemon thyme to serve.

Farro with Asparagus, Prosciutto, and Salsa Verde

SERVES 2
PREPARATION 10 MIN
COOKING 45 MIN

FOR THE SALSA VERDE
½ GARLIC CLOVE
1 TEASPOON CAPERS
1 TEASPOON DIJON MUSTARD
1 TEASPOON RED WINE VINEGAR
1 TABLESPOON CHOPPED BASIL
1 TABLESPOON CHOPPED
  FLAT-LEAF PARSLEY
1 TABLESPOON CHOPPED MINT
2 TABLESPOONS OLIVE OIL
SALT AND PEPPER

FOR THE PORRIDGE
2 TABLESPOONS OLIVE OIL
4 TABLESPOONS SLICED ONION
¾ CUP (5 OZ / 150 G) PEARLED ITALIAN
  FARRO (PEARLED SPELT)
1–2 SPLASHES DRY WHITE WINE
ABOUT 2½ CUPS (20 FL OZ / 600 ML)
  VEGETABLE BROTH (STOCK)
2 OZ / 50 G ASPARAGUS
2 TEASPOONS GRATED PARMESAN
1 TABLESPOON UNSALTED BUTTER
1½ OZ / 40 G PROSCIUTTO, SLICED
  INTO RIBBONS

First, make the salsa verde. Put all the ingredients into a food processor, pulse until the mixture resembles a coarse paste, and season to taste.

To make the porridge, place a medium pan over medium heat and add 1 tablespoon of the olive oil and the onion. Let the onion sweat for 1–2 minutes, then add the farro (pearled spelt) and a splash of white wine.

Pour in 2 cups (16 fl oz / 475 ml) of the broth (stock). Stir occasionally and cook for 40 minutes, or until the farro is tender. If it is not yet tender, continue to cook and add the remaining broth.

Chop the asparagus into thin slices but keep the tips whole. When almost all the broth has been absorbed, add the chopped asparagus to the pan and cook for 5 minutes. Stir in the Parmesan and the butter.

Meanwhile, fill a small pan with water, place over high heat and bring to a boil. Add the asparagus tips and blanch for 2 minutes. Remove with a slotted spoon and set aside.

Divide the farro and asparagus between 2 bowls. Top with the asparagus tips, prosciutto ribbons, and a spoonful of salsa verde to serve.

Farro with Roasted Venison, Mixed Beets, and Sauerkraut

SERVES 2
PREPARATION 15 MIN
COOKING AT LEAST 2–3 HRS

¼ TEASPOON GROUND CLOVES
¼ TEASPOON GROUND ALLSPICE
¼ TEASPOON GROUND NUTMEG
½ TEASPOON SALT
¼ TEASPOON GROUND BLACK PEPPER
1 LB 2 OZ / 500 G VENISON
  SHOULDER, DICED
2 TABLESPOONS RAPESEED OIL
2½ CUPS (20 FL OZ / 600 ML)
  HIGH-QUALITY RED WINE
1 TABLESPOON OLIVE OIL
2 GARLIC CLOVES, FINELY CHOPPED
1 SHALLOT, FINELY CHOPPED
2 SPRIGS THYME
¾ CUP (5 OZ / 150 G) PEARLED ITALIAN
  FARRO (PEARLED SPELT)
2 CUPS (16 FL OZ / 475 ML) BEEF
  BROTH (STOCK)
2 OZ / 50 G RAW BEETS (BEETROOT),
  THINLY SLICED
2 TABLESPOONS SAUERKRAUT,
  DRAINED
2 TABLESPOONS CRÈME FRAÎCHE
SALT AND BLACK PEPPER

Preheat the oven to 300°F/150°C/Gas Mark 2.

Mix the ground cloves, allspice, nutmeg, salt, and pepper in a bowl. Add the diced venison and rub it all over with the mixture.

Heat a heavy pan or a flame-proof Dutch oven (casserole dish) to a high heat and add the oil. Sear the venison on all sides for 2–3 minutes, until caramelized evenly. If using a Dutch oven, add 2 cups (16 fl oz / 475 ml) red wine, cover, and transfer to the oven.

Alternatively, if using a slow cooker, add the red wine and deglaze by scraping the cooking juices off the bottom of the pan with a wooden spoon or spatula (fish slice) and incorporating them into the wine. Transfer to the slow cooker and cook for at least 2–3 hours, or until the meat is falling apart.

Place a medium saucepan over medium heat. Add the olive oil, garlic, shallots, and thyme. Cook for 1 minute, then add the farro (pearled spelt). Cook for another 2 minutes, then add the broth (stock) and remaining ½ cup (4 fl oz / 120 ml) red wine. Bring to a simmer, cover, and cook over low heat for 40 minutes, or until the farro is tender.

Meanwhile, place a small pan over medium heat, add the beet (beetroot) slices and enough water to cover them. Cook for 10 minutes, or until the slices are tender, then drain and set aside.

Once the farro is tender, divide it between 2 bowls. Top with the venison, beet slices, sauerkraut, and crème fraîche. Season to taste with salt and pepper and serve.

Either preheat the oven to 275°F/140°C/Gas Mark 1 or set a slow cooker to the high setting.

Put the olive oil, red onion, and garlic into a medium pan and place over medium heat. Cook for 5–10 minutes, or until translucent, then transfer to a Dutch oven (casserole dish), if using the oven, or the slow cooker.

Return the pan to the heat, increase the heat to high, and sear the brisket on all sides. Place in the Dutch oven or slow cooker. Mix ⅓ cup (2½ fl oz / 75 ml) of the beef broth (stock), the balsamic vinegar, and brown sugar and pour over the beef. Cover and cook for 5–6 hours, or until extremely tender.

Allow the beef to rest either in the oven with the heat turned off, or in the slow cooker (also turned off) for 30 minutes.

When the beef is ready, put a medium pan over medium heat and add the wheat, kamut, and spelt flakes along with the remaining 3 cups (24 fl oz / 720 ml) beef broth. Cook for 7–8 minutes, or until all the liquid has been absorbed, then stir in half the watercress.

Divide the grains between 2 bowls. Shred the beef and pile it on top. Finish by spooning on some chimichurri sauce and sprinkle with the remaining watercress.

Wheat, Kamut, and Spelt with Slow-Cooked Brisket and Chimichurri Sauce

SERVES 2
PREPARATION 10 MIN
**COOKING 5–6 HRS, PLUS
30 MIN RESTING**

2 TABLESPOONS OLIVE OIL
7 OZ / 200 G RED ONION, SLICED
2 GARLIC CLOVES, MINCED
1 LB 2 OZ / 500 G BEEF BRISKET
3⅓ CUPS (28 FL OZ / 800 ML)
   BEEF BROTH (STOCK)
2 TABLESPOONS BALSAMIC VINEGAR
1 TABLESPOON BROWN SUGAR
1½ CUPS (5 OZ / 150 G) MIXED WHEAT,
   KAMUT, AND SPELT FLAKES
4 TABLESPOONS CHIMICHURRI SAUCE
2 CUPS (1½ OZ / 40 G) WATERCRESS,
   COARSELY CHOPPED

Vegetable Bowls

Millet with Kale, Mushrooms, and Pecorino

Place a heavy pan over medium heat and add 4 tablespoons of the butter. When it starts to foam, add the mushrooms. Move them as little as possible to give them color. Season to taste with salt and pepper and cook for 3–4 minutes. Remove from the pan and set aside.

Add the remaining butter to the pan, then add the shallot and garlic. Allow to cook for 1–2 minutes, then add the millet. After 2–3 more minutes add the white wine. Once the wine has been absorbed by the millet, add the broth (stock) and cook for 10–15 minutes, stirring occasionally as the liquid is absorbed. Season to taste.

When almost all the broth has been absorbed, add the kale and half the mushrooms and cook for 2–3 minutes.

Once the millet is cooked, divide between 2 bowls. Top with the remaining mushrooms and the pecorino shavings and drizzle with the truffle oil. Season with salt and pepper to serve.

SERVES 2
PREPARATION 10 MIN
COOKING 18–27 MIN

6 TABLESPOONS UNSALTED BUTTER
9 OZ / 250 G WILD OR CHESTNUT
  MUSHROOMS, COARSELY CUT
  INTO SIMILAR-SIZE PIECES
1 SHALLOT, FINELY CHOPPED
1 GARLIC CLOVE, FINELY CHOPPED
1 CUP (7 OZ / 200 G) MILLET
¼ CUP (2 FL OZ / 60 ML) WHITE WINE
2¾ CUPS (22 FL OZ / 660 ML)
  VEGETABLE BROTH (STOCK)
¾ CUP (2 OZ / 50 G) CHOPPED
  KALE LEAVES
2 TABLESPOONS PECORINO SHAVINGS
DRIZZLE OF TRUFFLE OIL
SALT AND BLACK PEPPER

Rye and Spelt with Roasted Garlic, Eggplant, and Feta

Preheat the oven to 350°F/180°C/Gas Mark 4. Line a baking sheet with parchment (baking) paper.

Put 3 tablespoons of the oil into a bowl, add the eggplant (aubergine) and garlic cloves and stir to coat. Arrange the eggplant and garlic on the prepared baking sheet and bake in the oven for 40 minutes, or until golden. Turn off the oven and leave the eggplant inside, but remove the garlic and crush.

Heat a medium pan over medium heat and add the remaining oil and the onion. Cook for 2–3 minutes, or until the onion is translucent. Add the grains, cook for 1 minute, then add the wine. Allow the wine to become absorbed then add the broth (stock) and garlic and season to taste with salt and pepper. Cook for 7–8 minutes. Once almost all the broth has been absorbed, add the lemon juice and three-quarters of the lemon zest. Remove from the heat and stir in the butter.

Divide the rye and spelt between 2 bowls. Top with the baked eggplant and crumbled feta. Sprinkle with the reserved lemon zest and a little parsley to serve.

SERVES 2
PREPARATION 5 MIN
COOKING 50 MIN

6 TABLESPOONS OLIVE OIL
1 EGGPLANT (AUBERGINE), CUT INTO
 ½ INCH / 1 CM DICE
4 GARLIC CLOVES
½ ONION, PEELED AND
 FINELY CHOPPED
1½ CUPS (5 OZ / 150 G) MIXED RYE
 AND SPELT FLAKES
¼ CUP (2 FL OZ / 60 ML) WHITE WINE
2½ CUPS (20 FL OZ / 600 ML)
 VEGETABLE BROTH (STOCK)
2 TABLESPOONS LEMON JUICE
GRATED ZEST OF ½ LEMON
3 TABLESPOONS BUTTER
3 TABLESPOONS CRUMBLED FETA
SALT AND BLACK PEPPER
CHOPPED PARSLEY, TO SPRINKLE

Farro with Slow-Roasted Tomatoes, Asparagus, and Hazelnuts

Preheat the oven to 350°F/180°C/Gas Mark 4.

Put the cherry tomatoes into a bowl with 1 tablespoon of the oil and season with salt and pepper. Toss to coat. Transfer to a small baking dish and bake in the oven for 30 minutes. After 25 minutes, sprinkle with the oregano and turn the tomatoes to coat. Remove from the oven and set aside.

Meanwhile, place a medium pan over medium heat and add the remaining oil and the onion. Let the onion sweat for 1–2 minutes, then add the farro (pearled spelt) and wine. Pour in enough broth (stock) to cover the farro. Cook for 40 minutes, stirring occasionally, or until the liquid is absorbed and the farro is tender. If it is not tender and soft, continue to cook and add more broth if required.

Chop the asparagus into slices but keep the tips whole. Add the chopped asparagus to the farro when almost all the broth has been absorbed. Cook for 5 minutes, then stir in the grated Parmesan.

Meanwhile, fill a small pan with water, place over high heat and bring to a boil. Add the asparagus tips and blanch for 2 minutes. Remove with a slotted spoon and set aside.

Divide the farro between 2 bowls. Top with the roasted tomatoes, asparagus tips, and chopped hazelnuts. Season with salt and pepper to serve.

SERVES 2
PREPARATION 5 MIN
COOKING 40 MIN

3 TABLESPOONS OLIVE OIL
⅔ CUP (3½ OZ / 100 G)
   CHERRY TOMATOES
1 TEASPOON OREGANO
¾ CUP (5 OZ / 150 G) PEARLED
   ITALIAN FARRO (PEARLED SPELT)
4 TABLESPOONS SLICED ONION
SPLASH OF DRY WHITE WINE
2½ CUPS (20 FL OZ / 600 ML)
   VEGETABLE BROTH (STOCK)
2 OZ / 50 G ASPARAGUS
4 TABLESPOONS GRATED PARMESAN
2 TEASPOONS CHOPPED HAZELNUTS
SALT AND BLACK PEPPER

Kamut with Truffle, Pickled Cucumber, and Radish Salsa

SERVES 2
PREPARATION 15 MIN, PLUS 1 HR SALTING AND 2 HRS PICKLING
COOKING 10 MIN

FOR THE PORRIDGE

1 TABLESPOON OLIVE OIL
1 TEASPOON BUTTER
½ OR 1 SMALL ONION, SLICED
1 LEEK, WHITE PART ONLY SLICED
  INTO FINE DISKS
¾ CUP (5 OZ / 150 G) KAMUT FLAKES
SPLASH OF DRY WHITE WINE
2½ CUPS (20 FL OZ / 600 ML)
  VEGETABLE BROTH (STOCK)
2 TEASPOONS GRATED BLACK TRUFFLE,
  OR 1 SMALL BLACK TRUFFLE,
  GRATED, OR A FEW DROPS OF
  WHITE TRUFFLE OIL
SALT AND BLACK PEPPER

FOR THE PICKLED CUCUMBER

4 INCH / 10 CM PIECE OF CUCUMBER,
  PEELED AND THINLY SLICED
2 TEASPOONS SEA SALT FLAKES
½ CUP (4 FL OZ / 120 ML) APPLE
  CIDER VINEGAR
2 TABLESPOONS GRANULATED SUGAR
½ TEASPOON CORIANDER SEEDS
½ TEASPOON YELLOW MUSTARD SEEDS
½ TEASPOON BLACK PEPPERCORNS

FOR THE RADISH SALSA

1 TEASPOON FINELY CHOPPED
  CILANTRO (CORIANDER)
2 RADISHES, TRIMMED AND
  FINELY CHOPPED
1 SCALLION (SPRING ONION), WHITE
  PART ONLY, THINLY SLICED
¼ MILD CHILE, SEEDS REMOVED
  AND FINELY CHOPPED
1 TEASPOON FRESH LEMON JUICE

To make the pickled cucumber, mix the cucumber with the sea salt in a bowl, cover with plastic wrap (clingfilm), and set aside for 1 hour. Rinse under cold water, squeeze out any excess water, and place in a heatproof bowl.

Put the cider vinegar, sugar, coriander seeds, mustard seeds, and peppercorns in a small pan. Cook over medium heat for 2–3 minutes, or until the sugar has dissolved. Bring to a boil, then pour the mixture over the cucumber slices. Let cool, then refrigerate for at least 2 hours.

In a small bowl, mix together the ingredients for the radish salsa, cover, and set aside.

To make the porridge, place a medium pan over medium heat, add 1 tablespoon of the oil, 1 teaspoon of the butter, the onion, and leek and sweat for 1–2 minutes. Add the kamut and white wine. Pour in the broth (stock) and cook for 6–8 minutes, or until it has all been absorbed and the kamut is tender. Season to taste with salt and pepper. Remove from the heat.

Divide the kamut between 2 bowls. Drain the pickled cucumber and spoon over the kamut. Top with the radish salsa and sprinkle with the truffle or drizzle with the truffle oil, if using.

Place a medium pan over high heat, add the broth (stock) and bring to a boil. Add the kohlrabi and cook for about 5 minutes, or until tender. Remove the kohlrabi with a slotted spoon and set aside. Keep the broth warm.

Place another pan over medium heat and add the olive oil and the onion. Sweat the onion for 1–2 minutes. Pour in the wine and cook for another minute, then add the spelt flakes. Pour in the broth and cook for 7–8 minutes, stirring occasionally, or until it has been absorbed. Season to taste with salt and pepper and stir in the kohlrabi and parsley.

Divide the spelt between 2 bowls. Top with the pickled walnuts, cauliflower, or cipollini onions, and the crumbled Roquefort to serve.

Spelt with Kohlrabi and Roquefort

SERVES 2
PREPARATION 10 MIN
COOKING 20 MIN

3 CUPS (24 FL OZ / 720 ML)
  VEGETABLE BROTH (STOCK)
1 X 11 OZ / 300 G KOHLRABI, PEELED
  AND CUT INTO ½ INCH / 1 CM CUBES
  (ABOUT 2 CUPS)
2 TABLESPOONS OLIVE OIL
1 ONION, FINELY DICED
4 TABLESPOONS DRY WHITE WINE
1½ CUPS (5 OZ / 150 G) SPELT FLAKES
1 TEASPOON FINELY CHOPPED PARSLEY
4 PICKLED WALNUTS, CHOPPED, OR
  SWEET PICKLED CAULIFLOWER
  OR CIPOLLINI ONIONS
2 TABLESPOONS CRUMBLED ROQUEFORT
SALT AND BLACK PEPPER

Farro with Beets, Feta, Poached Eggs, and Capers

Put 9 oz / 250 g of the cooked beets (beetroot) into a food processor and process to a puree. Cut the remaining beets into medium dice.

Place a medium pan over medium heat, add the oil and farro (pearled spelt). Stir and cook for 2 minutes. Add the Madeira and the broth (stock). Cook for 20 minutes, stirring occasionally, until almost all the liquid has been absorbed. Add the beet puree and cook for 5–10 minutes, or until that also has been almost all absorbed.

When the beet mixture is almost ready, bring a pan of water to a simmer over medium heat, add the vinegar and swirl the water clockwise with a spoon to create a whirlpool. Crack the eggs and drop them, one at a time, into the center of the swirling water but make sure they do not touch each other. The eggs should take 2–3 minutes to cook. The fresher the eggs, the more likely they are to form a perfectly poached egg. Use a slotted spoon to prod an egg white to see if it's firm; if it is then immediately remove the eggs from the water and set aside on a plate lined with paper towels.

Divide the beet farro between 2 bowls. Top with the poached eggs, cubed feta, and diced beets and scatter with the capers. Season with salt and pepper to serve.

SERVES 2
PREPARATION 10 MIN
COOKING 30–35 MIN

11 OZ / 300 G COOKED BEETS
　(BEETROOT), NOT IN VINEGAR
2 TABLESPOONS VEGETABLE OIL
¾ CUP (5 OZ / 150 G) PEARLED ITALIAN
　FARRO (PEARLED SPELT)
SPLASH OF MADEIRA
1¼ CUPS (10 FL OZ / 300 ML) WARM
　VEGETABLE BROTH (STOCK)
2 EGGS
2 TABLESPOONS WHITE WINE VINEGAR
2 OZ / 50 G FETA, CUBED
1 TABLESPOON CAPERS
SALT AND BLACK PEPPER

Farro with Cauliflower, Girolles, and Mascarpone

SERVES 2
PREPARATION 5 MIN
COOKING 35 MIN

⅔ CUP (5 FL OZ / 150 ML) HEAVY
  (DOUBLE) CREAM
⅔ CUP (5 FL OZ / 150 ML) WHOLE
  (FULL-FAT) MILK
5 OZ / 150 G CAULIFLOWER FLORETS
4 TABLESPOONS UNSALTED BUTTER
2 TABLESPOONS FINELY CHOPPED
  SHALLOT
¾ CUP (5 OZ / 150 G) PEARLED ITALIAN
  FARRO (PEARLED SPELT)
2 CUPS 16 FL OZ / 475 ML)
  VEGETABLE BROTH (STOCK)
1 TEASPOON FINELY CHOPPED THYME
5 OZ / 150 G GIROLLES OR WILD
  MUSHROOMS
2 TABLESPOONS MASCARPONE
2 TEASPOONS FINELY CHOPPED CHIVES
SALT AND BLACK PEPPER

Place a medium pan over medium heat, pour in the cream and the milk, and bring to a boil. Add the cauliflower florets and a big pinch of salt. Simmer for 5 minutes, or until the cauliflower is soft. Strain the cauliflower, transfer to a food processor, and process until a puree.

Heat 2 teaspoons of the butter in a medium pan over medium heat and fry the shallots for 2–3 minutes, or until softened. Add the farro (pearled spelt) and stir to coat with the butter and shallots. Add the broth (stock) and thyme and cook for 20 minutes, stirring occasionally, until almost all the liquid has been absorbed.

Add the cauliflower puree and continue to cook until the farro is soft. You may need to add more broth until the farro reaches the desired consistency. Remove from the heat and season to taste with salt and pepper.

Meanwhile, place a skillet (frying pan) over medium-high heat. Add the remaining butter and fry the girolles or wild mushrooms for 5–8 minutes, allowing them to color. Season to taste with salt and pepper.

Divide the farro between 2 bowls. Top with the girolles and a spoonful of the mascarpone. Sprinkle with the chives to serve.

Buckwheat with Roasted Pumpkin, Madeira, and Carrots

Preheat the oven to 350°F/180°C/Gas Mark 4. Line a baking sheet with parchment (baking) paper.

Put the pumpkin sticks on the prepared baking sheet. Drizzle with oil and season with salt and pepper. Roast in the oven for 25 minutes.

Meanwhile, in a medium pan, melt the butter over medium heat. Add the onion, stir for 2–3 minutes, or until softened, then add the buckwheat. Pour in the Madeira and cook for 3 minutes, or until it has been absorbed. Pour in the broth (stock) and cook for about 20 minutes, or until it has been absorbed.

Stir in both the cheeses, season to taste with salt and pepper, and remove from the heat.

Divide the buckwheat between 2 bowls. Using a vegetable peeler, peel thin strands of the carrot onto the buckwheat. Top with the roasted pumpkin, drizzle with extra virgin olive oil, and sprinkle with the thyme to serve.

SERVES 2
PREPARATION 10 MIN
COOKING 30 MIN

1 CUP (4 OZ / 120 G) PUMPKIN, CUT
  INTO SHORT STICKS
1 TABLESPOON OLIVE OIL
2 TABLESPOONS UNSALTED BUTTER
1 SMALL ONION, FINELY CHOPPED
1 CUP (6 OZ / 175 G) BUCKWHEAT
⅔ CUP (5 FL OZ / 150 ML) MADEIRA
2½ CUPS (18 FL OZ / 550 ML)
  VEGETABLE BROTH (STOCK)
4 TABLESPOONS FINELY
  GRATED PECORINO
4 TABLESPOONS FINELY
  GRATED PARMESAN
2 SMALL CARROTS
EXTRA VIRGIN OLIVE OIL,
  FOR DRIZZLING
1 TEASPOON FINELY CHOPPED THYME
SALT AND BLACK PEPPER

Wheat, Barley, and Rye with Braised Red Cabbage, Lima Beans, and Gruyère

SERVES 2
PREPARATION 10 MIN
COOKING 1 HR

FOR THE PORRIDGE
1 TABLESPOON OLIVE OIL
½ ONION, FINELY CHOPPED
1 GARLIC CLOVE, FINELY CHOPPED
1 TEASPOON PAPRIKA
1 TEASPOON DRIED OREGANO
1 SMALL RED CHILE, FINELY DICED
1½ CUPS (5 OZ / 150 G) MIXED WHEAT,
   RYE, AND BARLEY FLAKES
3 CUPS (24 FL OZ / 720 ML)
   VEGETABLE BROTH (STOCK)
¼ CUP (2 OZ / 50 G) LIMA
   (BUTTER) BEANS
4 TABLESPOONS LEMON JUICE
6 TABLESPOONS GRATED GRUYÈRE
2 TEASPOONS FINELY
   CHOPPED PARSLEY
SALT AND PEPPER

FOR THE BRAISED CABBAGE
2 TEASPOONS UNSALTED BUTTER
3½ OZ / 100 G RED CABBAGE,
   FINELY GRATED OR CHOPPED
4 TEASPOON RED WINE VINEGAR
6 TABLESPOONS RED WINE
2 TEASPOONS SUPERFINE
   (CASTER) SUGAR

To make the braised red cabbage, put a medium pan over medium heat and add the butter. Once it foams, add the red cabbage and the rest of the ingredients. Reduce the heat to very low and cook for 1 hour.

To make the porridge, place a heavy pan over medium heat and add the olive oil, onion, garlic, paprika, oregano, and chile. After 2–3 minutes add the grains and cook for 3–4 minutes, stirring constantly to prevent burning. Pour in the broth (stock), add the fava (butter) beans, and season to taste with salt and pepper. Cook for 7–8 minutes, or until all the liquid has been absorbed and the grains are soft. Stir in the lemon juice and 4 tablespoons of the Gruyère. Remove from the heat.

Divide the porridge between 2 bowls. Top with the braised red cabbage and sprinkle with the parsley and remaining Gruyère to serve.

Rye and Barley with Sweet Peppers, Arugula, and Chile

Place a heavy pan over medium heat and add 1 tablespoon of the olive oil, the oregano, chile, onion, and garlic and sweat for 2–3 minutes. Add the grains and cook for 3–4 minutes, stirring constantly to prevent the grains from burning.

Pour in the broth (stock), add the lemon zest, and season with salt to taste. Reduce the heat to low and simmer for 7–8 minutes, or until all the liquid has been absorbed and the grains are soft.

Divide the rye and barley between 2 bowls. Top with the sweet pepper strands, arugula (rocket), and the lemon wedges to serve.

SERVES 2
PREPARATION 5 MIN
COOKING 12–13 MIN

4 TABLESPOONS OLIVE OIL
1 TEASPOON DRIED OREGANO
1 SMALL RED CHILE, FINELY DICED
½ ONION, FINELY CHOPPED
1 GARLIC CLOVE, FINELY CHOPPED
1½ CUPS (5 OZ / 150 G) MIXED RYE
   AND BARLEY FLAKES
2½ CUPS (20 FL OZ / 600 ML)
   VEGETABLE BROTH (STOCK)
1 TEASPOON FINELY GRATED
   LEMON ZEST
2 SWEET PEPPERS (PRESERVED),
   CUT INTO LONG STRANDS
1 SMALL HANDFUL OF
   ARUGULA (ROCKET)
2 LEMON WEDGES
SALT AND BLACK PEPPER

Indulgent
Sweet Bowls

4-Grain Porridge with Spiced Plums and Hazelnut Crumble

Serves 2
Preparation 15 min
Cooking 20 min

4 PLUMS, HALVED, PITS
  (STONES) REMOVED
JUICE OF 1 ORANGE
½ TEASPOON STEVIA OR
  2 TABLESPOONS PACKED
  BROWN SUGAR
½ TEASPOON GROUND CINNAMON
¼ TEASPOON EACH GROUND
  CARDAMOM, NUTMEG, AND
  BLACK PEPPER
½ CUP (3 OZ / 80 G) HAZELNUTS
2 TABLESPOONS BUCKWHEAT FLOUR
2 TABLESPOONS CACAO NIBS
½ TEASPOON STEVIA OR 2 TEASPOONS
  SUPERFINE (CASTER) SUGAR
4 TEASPOONS COCONUT OIL
¼ CUP (1 OZ / 25 G) BARLEY FLAKES
¼ CUP (1 OZ / 25 G) WHEAT FLAKES
¼ CUP (1 OZ / 25 G) RYE FLAKES
¼ CUP (1 OZ / 25 G) SPELT FLAKES
1½ CUPS (12 FL OZ / 350 ML)
  COCONUT MILK BEVERAGE
2 TEASPOONS FLAXSEED (LINSEED)
1 TABLESPOON LIGHT (SINGLE)
  CREAM (OPTIONAL)

Preheat the oven to 400°F/200°C/Gas Mark 6. Line 2 small baking dishes with parchment (baking) paper.

Put the plum halves, cut-side up, into one of the baking dishes. Whisk together the orange juice, stevia or brown sugar, cinnamon, cardamom, nutmeg, and pepper in a bowl and drizzle the mixture over the plums.

To make the crumble topping, put the hazelnuts into a food processor and pulse once or twice before adding the buckwheat flour, cacao nibs, stevia or superfine (caster) sugar, and coconut oil. Pulse until the texture resembles bread crumbs. Put the crumble mixture into the second baking dish.

Bake both dishes for 20 minutes. The plums should be bubbling and the crumble mixture should be turning golden brown.

Meanwhile, put the barley flakes, wheat flakes, rye flakes, and spelt flakes into a medium pan, pour in the coconut milk and 1½ cups (12 fl oz / 350 ml) water and place over high heat. Bring to a boil. Once the liquid has begun to reduce, stir quickly to prevent the porridge from sticking. Reduce to medium-high heat and cook for 7–8 minutes, or until the porridge reaches the desired consistency, then remove from the heat.

Divide the porridge between 2 bowls. Top with the plums, crumble topping, and flaxseed (linseed). Drizzle with a little cream, if using, and serve.

Oats with Quinoa Shortbread, Baked Apple, and Vanilla Cream

SERVES 2
PREPARATION 15 MIN
COOKING 40 MIN

1 CUP (3½ OZ / 100 G) ROLLED OATS
1½ CUPS (12 FL OZ / 350 ML)
   ALMOND MILK
¼ TEASPOON GROUND CINNAMON

FOR THE QUINOA SHORTBREAD
1 TABLESPOON QUINOA
3 TABLESPOONS ALL-PURPOSE
   (PLAIN) FLOUR
2 TABLESPOONS DARK BROWN SUGAR
½ TEASPOON SALT
1½ TABLESPOONS UNSALTED BUTTER,
   COLD AND CUBED

FOR THE BAKED APPLE
½ TEASPOON GRANULATED SUGAR
   (OPTIONAL)
1 GALA OR OTHER SWEET APPLE
¼ TEASPOON LEMON JUICE

FOR THE VANILLA CREAM
2 TABLESPOONS WHIPPING CREAM
½ TEASPOON CONFECTIONERS'
   (ICING) SUGAR
¼ TEASPOON VANILLA BEAN PASTE

To make the quinoa shortbread, place a small nonstick pan over medium-low heat. Add the quinoa and allow it to toast, stirring often, for 5 minutes, or until it is popping. Transfer to a plate and let cool.

Preheat the oven to 350°F/180°C/Gas Mark 4. Grease and line a baking sheet and a small baking pan with parchment (baking) paper.

Put the cooled quinoa into a food processor and pulse for 1 minute. Add the flour, brown sugar, and salt and pulse to combine. Add the butter and pulse until the dough comes together in a large clump.

Press the quinoa shortbread dough into the prepared pan so that it forms a ½ inch / 1 cm thick, even layer. Don't worry if there isn't enough dough to fill the pan; just try to make a square or rectangle shape. Sprinkle evenly with granulated sugar, if using.

To make the baked apple, cut the apple in half and rub the exposed sides with lemon juice, then lay them cut-side up on the prepared baking sheet. Put it and the shortbread dough into the oven.

Bake the shortbread for 25–30 minutes, or until lightly browned. Remove from the oven and immediately score the shortbread lengthwise into 2 evenly sized pieces; break apart. The apple should be ready after 30 minutes, or when it is soft when poked with a fork. Remove from the oven.

Meanwhile, to make the vanilla cream, put the cream, confectioners' (icing) sugar, and vanilla into a bowl and whisk until stiff peaks form. Set aside.

Put the oats into a medium pan, add the almond milk and 1½ cups (12 fl oz / 350 ml) water and place over high heat. Bring to a boil. Once the liquid has begun to reduce, stir quickly to prevent the porridge from sticking. Cook over medium-high heat for 5 minutes, or until the porridge reaches the desired consistency. Remove from the heat.

Divide the oats between 2 bowls. Top with the shortbread and the baked apple and drizzle with the vanilla cream. Dust with cinnamon to serve.

Millet and Rye with Banana, Kinder Schocko-Bons, and Dried Cranberry

Put the millet into a medium pan, pour in the coconut milk beverage and 1½ cups (12 fl oz / 350 ml) water and place over high heat. Bring to a boil, then reduce the heat to medium-low, cover, and simmer for 18–20 minutes, stirring as the liquid is absorbed.

Meanwhile, thinly slice the banana at an angle to get slightly larger disks. Cut the chocolate into bite-size pieces. Set aside.

Add the rye flakes to the pan and increase the heat to medium. You may need to add up to ¼ cup (2 fl oz / 60 ml) more water if the millet absorbs a lot of liquid. Cook, stirring, for 7–8 minutes, or until the desired consistency is reached. Remove from the heat and stir in the cinnamon and cloves.

Divide the millet and rye between 2 bowls. Top with the banana slices and chocolate pieces. Sprinkle with the dried cranberry and drizzle with the maple syrup to serve.

SERVES 2
PREPARATION 2 MIN
COOKING 26–28 MIN

⅓ CUP (2½ OZ 65 G) MILLET
1½ CUPS (12 FL OZ / 350 ML) COCONUT
   MILK BEVERAGE
1 BANANA
10–20 KINDER SCHOCKO-BONS,
   4 KINDER MAXI BARS, OR LINDT
   LINDOR MILK TRUFFLES
½ CUP (2 OZ / 50 G) RYE FLAKES
½ TEASPOON GROUND CINNAMON
¼ TEASPOON GROUND CLOVES
½ TEASPOON DRIED
   CRANBERRY POWDER
2 TABLESPOONS MAPLE SYRUP

To make the peanut brittle, first line a small plate with parchment (baking) paper. Put the butter and sugar into a small pan over medium heat. Allow to bubble until the mixture turns golden brown but is not burned. Add the peanuts and coat them thoroughly. Transfer to the prepared plate and allow to cool completely, then put into a food processor and pulse until the mixture resembles bread crumbs.

Put the raspberries and confectioners' (icing) sugar into a food processor and pulse until the fruit liquefies. Pass the fruit through a fine strainer (sieve) to remove the seeds, then reserve the resulting coulis. Set aside.

Put the barley flakes and spelt flakes into a medium pan, pour in the coconut milk and 1½ cups (12 fl oz / 350 ml) water and bring to a boil. Once the liquid has begun to reduce, stir quickly to prevent the porridge from sticking. Reduce to medium-high heat and cook for 7–8 minutes, or until the porridge reaches the desired consistency, then remove from the heat.

Divide between 2 bowls. Top with the chocolate spread, sprinkle with the peanut brittle powder, and spoon over the raspberry coulis to serve.

Barley and Spelt with Nutella, Peanut Brittle, and Raspberry Coulis

SERVES 2
PREPARATION 5 MIN
COOKING 25 MIN

2 TEASPOONS UNSALTED BUTTER
4 TEASPOONS SUPERFINE
  (CASTER) SUGAR
3 TABLESPOONS ROASTED LIGHTLY
  SALTED PEANUTS
½ CUP (2¼ OZ / 60 G) RASPBERRIES
1 TEASPOON CONFECTIONERS'
  (ICING) SUGAR
½ CUP (2 OZ / 50 G) BARLEY FLAKES
½ CUP (2 OZ / 50 G) SPELT FLAKES
1½ CUPS (12 FL OZ / 350 ML) COCONUT
  MILK BEVERAGE
2 TABLESPOONS CHOCOLATE SPREAD
  SUCH AS NUTELLA

Quinoa and Oats with Chocolate, Raspberries, and Lime Mousse

SERVES 2
PREPARATION 10 MIN
COOKING 22 MIN

½ TEASPOON GRATED LIME ZEST,
  PLUS EXTRA TO SPRINKLE
2 TABLESPOONS FRESH LIME JUICE
1½ TABLESPOONS SUPERFINE
  (CASTER) SUGAR
SMALL PINCH OF SALT
1 EGG
1½ TABLESPOONS UNSALTED
  BUTTER, DICED
2½ TABLESPOONS CHILLED
  WHIPPING CREAM
2 OZ / 50 G BITTERSWEET (DARK)
  CHOCOLATE (MINIMUM 70%
  COCOA SOLIDS)
⅓ CUP (2¼ OZ / 60 G) QUINOA
1½ CUPS (12 FL OZ / 350 ML)
  ALMOND MILK
½ CUP (2 OZ / 50 G) ROLLED OATS
½ CUP (2¼ OZ / 60 G) RASPBERRIES

Mix together the lime zest, lime juice, sugar, salt, and egg in a small heavy pan to make a custard base for the mousse. Add the butter and place over medium-low heat. Cook, whisking frequently, for about 5 minutes, or until thick enough to coat the back of a spoon.

Push the custard mixture through a fine strainer (sieve) set over a bowl. Place this bowl in another, slightly larger, bowl filled with ice. Leave for 5 minutes, stirring occasionally.

In a small bowl, beat the cream with a whisk until it holds stiff peaks, then gently fold into the custard. Set aside.

Grate the chocolate finely.

Put the quinoa into a medium pan, pour in the almond milk and 1½ cups (12 fl oz / 350 ml) water and place over low heat. Bring to a simmer, cover, and cook for 15 minutes. Add the oats and grated chocolate and increase the heat to medium. You may need to add up to ¼ cup (2 fl oz / 60 ml) more water if the quinoa absorbs a lot of liquid. Cook, stirring, for 5 minutes, or until the porridge reaches the desired consistency. Remove from the heat.

Divide the chocolate quinoa and oats between 2 bowls. Top with the raspberries and spoon over as much or as little of the mousse as desired. Sprinkle with lime zest to serve.

Millet, Quinoa, and Oats with Strawberries, Peaches, and Mint

Put the millet and quinoa into a medium pan, pour in the almond milk and 1 cup (8 fl oz / 250 ml) water and place over medium heat. Bring to a simmer, cover, and cook for 15 minutes.

Add the oats and cook for another 7–8 minutes, or until the porridge reaches the desired consistency. You may need to add up to ½ cup (4 fl oz / 120 ml) water if the grains have absorbed a lot of liquid. Remove from the heat and stir in the chopped mint.

Divide the porridge between 2 bowls. Top with the peach and strawberries. Sprinkle with mint strips and the flaked almonds and drizzle with the honey. Whisk the cream to form soft peaks and spoon it over to serve.

SERVES 2
PREPARATION 5 MIN
COOKING 23 MIN

⅓ CUP (2¼ OZ / 60 G) MILLET
4 TABLESPOONS (1½ OZ / 40 G) QUINOA
1 CUP (8 FL OZ / 250 ML) ALMOND MILK
⅓ CUP (1¼ OZ / 35 G) ROLLED OATS
8 MINT LEAVES, ½ CHOPPED AND
   ½ CUT INTO FINE STRIPS
1 RIPE PEACH, PITTED (STONED) AND
   CUT INTO ½ INCH (1 CM) CHUNKS
1 CUP (3½ OZ / 100 G) STRAWBERRIES,
   HULLED AND THINLY SLICED
4 TABLESPOONS FLAKED ALMONDS
2 TABLESPOONS HONEY
2 TABLESPOONS WHIPPING CREAM

Baked Porridge

Preheat the oven to 350°F/180°C/Gas Mark 4.

In a mixing bowl, combine the oats, vanilla, cinnamon, raisins, chopped apple, mixed peel, and orange zest and mix well. Stir in the milk and cream, then pour the mixture into 2 ovenproof bowls. Dust with a little extra cinnamon.

Put in the oven and bake for 30–35 minutes, or until all the liquid has been absorbed. Remove from the oven.

Brush the apricot jam over the top of each bowl of porridge and top with the apple slices. Sprinkle with the whiskey, if using, to serve.

SERVES 2
PREPARATION 3 MIN
COOKING 35 MIN

¾ CUP (3 OZ / 80 G) ROLLED OATS
½ TEASPOON VANILLA BEAN PASTE
2 TEASPOONS GROUND CINNAMON,
   PLUS EXTRA FOR SPRINKLING
2 TABLESPOONS GOLDEN RAISINS
   (SULTANAS)
1 APPLE, ½ FINELY CHOPPED AND
   ½ THINLY SLICED
2 TEASPOONS MIXED PEEL
1 TEASPOON GRATED ORANGE ZEST
1 CUP (8 FL OZ / 250 ML) WHOLE
   (FULL-FAT) MILK (ALTERNATIVELY,
   USE ALMOND OR COCONUT
   MILK BEVERAGE)
½ CUP (4 FL OZ / 120 ML) HEAVY
   (DOUBLE) CREAM (ALTERNATIVELY,
   USE ALMOND OR COCONUT MILK
   BEVERAGE)
2 TABLESPOONS APRICOT
   JAM (OPTIONAL)
2 TABLESPOONS WHISKEY (OPTIONAL)

Oats and Spelt with Milka and Daim Bar, Blueberries, and Raspberries

Put the oats and spelt flakes into a medium pan, pour in the coconut milk beverage and 1½ cups (12 fl oz / 350 ml) water and place over high heat. Bring to a boil. Once the liquid has begun to reduce, stir quickly to prevent the porridge from sticking. Reduce to medium-high heat and cook for 7–8 minutes, or until the porridge reaches the desired consistency. Remove from the heat.

Divide the oats and spelt between 2 bowls. Top with the chocolate and berries and sprinkle with the flaxseed (linseed) to serve.

SERVES 2
PREPARATION 2 MIN
COOKING 7–8 MIN

½ CUP (2 OZ / 50 G) ROLLED OATS
½ CUP (2 OZ / 50 G) SPELT FLAKES
1½ CUPS (12 FL OZ / 350 ML)
  COCONUT MILK BEVERAGE
2 OZ / 50 G MILKA AND DAIM BAR,
  HERSHEY'S SKOR, OR HEATH
  TOFFEE BAR, CHOPPED
¼ CUP (1 OZ / 25 G) BLUEBERRIES
¼ CUP (1¼ OZ / 30 G) RASPBERRIES
2 TEASPOONS FLAXSEED (LINSEED)

Pour the cream, whiskey, and sugar into a bowl and whisk just until the mixture forms stiff peaks.

Put the kamut flakes, wheat flakes, and barley flakes into a medium pan, pour in the coconut milk beverage and 1½ cups (12 fl oz / 350 ml) water and place over high heat. Bring to a boil. Once the liquid has begun to reduce, stir quickly to prevent the porridge from sticking. Reduce to medium-high heat and cook for 7–8 minutes, or until the porridge reaches the desired consistency, then stir in the marmalade. Remove from the heat.

Divide the porridge between 2 bowls. Top with the orange slices and spoon on as much of the whiskey cream as desired to serve.

Kamut, Wheat, and Barley with Seville Orange Marmalade, and Whiskey Cream

SERVES 2
PREPARATION 10 MIN
COOKING 7–8 MIN

½ CUP (4 FL OZ / 120 ML)
 HEAVY (DOUBLE) CREAM
2 TEASPOONS WHISKEY
½ TEASPOON CONFECTIONERS'
 (ICING) SUGAR
⅓ CUP (1¼ OZ / 35 G) KAMUT FLAKES
⅓ CUP (1¼ OZ / 35 G) WHEAT FLAKES
⅓ CUP (1¼ OZ / 35 G) BARLEY FLAKES
1½ CUPS (12 FL OZ / 350 ML)
 COCONUT MILK BEVERAGE
4 TABLESPOONS HIGH-QUALITY SEVILLE
 ORANGE MARMALADE
1 ORANGE, PEELED AND CUT
 INTO THIN DISKS

Oats and Wheat with Clementine, Mango, Blueberries, and Raspberry Coulis

Put the raspberries and confectioners' (icing) sugar into a mini blender or food processor and pulse until you get a smooth coulis. Set aside.

Put the whipping cream into a small bowl and whisk with an electric mixer or whisk until it forms soft peaks. Add the vanilla bean paste and whisk until combined. Set aside.

Put the oats and wheat flakes into a medium pan, pour in the coconut milk beverage and 1½ cups (12 fl oz / 350 ml) water and place over high heat. Bring to a boil. Once the liquid has begun to reduce, stir quickly to prevent the porridge from sticking. Reduce to medium-high heat and cook for 8–10 minutes or until the porridge reaches the desired consistency. Remove from the heat.

Divide the oats and wheat between 2 bowls. Top with the clementine segments, mango, blueberries, pistachios, and vanilla cream. Drizzle with the raspberry coulis and dust with confectioners' sugar to serve.

SERVES 2
PREPARATION 5 MIN
COOKING 8 MIN

½ CUP (2¼ OZ / 60 G) RASPBERRIES
½ TEASPOON CONFECTIONERS'
  (ICING) SUGAR, PLUS EXTRA
  FOR DUSTING
2 TABLESPOONS WHIPPING CREAM
¼ TEASPOON VANILLA BEAN PASTE
½ CUP (2 OZ / 50 G) ROLLED OATS
½ CUP (2 OZ / 50 G) WHEAT FLAKES
1½ CUPS (12 FL OZ / 350 ML) COCONUT
  MILK BEVERAGE
5–6 CLEMENTINE SEGMENTS, PEELED
½ MANGO, THINLY SLICED
2 TABLESPOONS BLUEBERRIES
1 TABLESPOON PISTACHIOS

Oat and Wheat Black Forest Porridge

Put the kirsch, cream, sugar, and vanilla into a bowl and whisk until the mixture forms stiff peaks.

Put the oats and wheat flakes into a medium pan, pour in the coconut milk and 1½ cups (12 fl oz / 350 ml) water and bring to a boil. Once the liquid has begun to reduce, stir quickly to prevent the porridge from sticking. Reduce to medium-high heat and cook for 7–8 minutes, or until the porridge reaches the desired consistency. Remove from the heat and stir in half the chocolate until combined.

Divide the porridge between 2 bowls. Top with the cherries and the cream mixture. Grate over the remaining chocolate to serve.

Serves 2
Preparation 5 min
Cooking 7–8 min

2 TABLESPOONS KIRSCH
2 TABLESPOONS WHIPPING CREAM
½ TEASPOON CONFECTIONERS'
  (ICING) SUGAR
¼ TEASPOON VANILLA BEAN PASTE
½ CUP (2 OZ / 50 G) ROLLED OATS
½ CUP (2 OZ / 50 G) WHEAT FLAKES
1½ CUPS (12 FL OZ / 350 ML) COCONUT
  MILK BEVERAGE
¼ CUP (1 OZ / 30 G) CHERRIES, HALVED
  AND PITTED (STONED), OR
  AMARENA CHERRIES, HALVED
1 OZ / 25 G BITTERSWEET (DARK)
  CHOCOLATE

Rye, Wheat, and Spelt with Salted Caramel, Balsamic Orange, and Brandy Snaps

Place a heavy pan over medium heat. Add the sugar and liquid glucose and heat until the mixture becomes an amber-colored caramel. Do not be tempted to shake the pan or stir the caramel initially.

Gradually pour in the cream and mix well. Remove from the heat and gradually stir in the butter, along with the sea salt. Set aside.

Place a small pan over medium heat. Add the balsamic vinegar, then the orange segments or slices and allow to glaze for a moment. Remove from the heat.

Put the rye, wheat, and spelt flakes into a medium pan, pour in the almond milk and 1½ cups (12 fl oz / 350 ml) water and place over high heat. Bring to a boil. Once the liquid has begun to reduce, stir quickly to prevent the porridge from sticking. Reduce to medium-high heat and cook for 10 minutes or until the porridge reaches the desired consistency. Remove from the heat.

Divide the porridge between 2 bowls. Top with the orange pieces and brandy snaps, then drizzle with as much of the salted caramel to serve.

SERVES 2
PREPARATION 2 MIN
COOKING 15–20 MIN

2½ TABLESPOONS SUPERFINE
  (CASTER) SUGAR
1 TEASPOON LIQUID GLUCOSE
1½ TABLESPOONS WHIPPING CREAM
2 TABLESPOONS UNSALTED BUTTER,
  AT ROOM TEMPERATURE
PINCH OF SEA SALT
½ TEASPOON BALSAMIC VINEGAR
½ AN ORANGE, PEELED AND
  SEGMENTED OR SLICED
½ CUP (2 OZ / 50 G) RYE FLAKES
¼ CUP (1 OZ / 25 G) WHEAT FLAKES
¼ CUP (1 OZ / 25 G) SPELT FLAKES
1½ CUPS (12 FL OZ / 350 ML)
  ALMOND MILK
2 HIGH-QUALITY BRANDY SNAPS

4-Grain Porridge with Candied Nuts, Cardamom, Banana, and Pumpkin Seeds

SERVES 2
PREPARATION 5 MIN
COOKING 40 MIN

4 TEASPOONS GRANULATED SUGAR
4 TEASPOONS LIGHT BROWN SUGAR
¼ TEASPOON GROUND CINNAMON
¼ TEASPOON SALT
2 TEASPOONS EGG WHITE
½ TEASPOON VANILLA BEAN PASTE
½ CUP (2¼ OZ / 60 G) MIX OF
   PECANS, WALNUTS, HAZELNUTS,
   AND CASHEW NUTS
1 BANANA
½ TEASPOON GROUND CARDAMOM
¼ CUP (1 OZ / 25 G) ROLLED OATS
¼ CUP (1 OZ / 25 G) WHEAT FLAKES
¼ CUP (1 OZ / 25 G) RYE FLAKES
¼ CUP (1 OZ / 25 G) BARLEY FLAKES
1½ CUPS (12 FL OZ / 350 ML)
   COCONUT MILK BEVERAGE
2 TEASPOONS TOASTED
   PUMPKIN SEEDS

Preheat the oven to 300°F/150°C/Gas Mark 2. Line a large baking sheet with parchment (baking) paper and set aside.

In a mixing bowl combine both sugars, the cinnamon, and salt. Set aside.

In a separate bowl whisk the egg white, vanilla, and a few drops of water together until frothy. Add the nuts and gently toss until they are well coated. Add the sugar and cinnamon mixture and toss until all the nuts are coated.

Spread the nuts out in a single layer on the baking sheet and bake for 40 minutes, stirring and turning them every 15 minutes. Remove from the oven and let cool on the baking sheet.

Meanwhile, cut the banana lengthwise to form 2 long pieces, then repeat to form 4 long pieces. Put a nonstick skillet (frying pan) over medium heat. Once hot, add the banana pieces and allow to caramelize a little before dusting with the cardamom. Remove from the heat.

Put the oats, wheat flakes, rye flakes, and barley flakes in a medium pan, add the coconut milk and 1½ cups (12 fl oz / 350 ml) water and place over high heat. Bring to a boil. Once the liquid has begun to reduce, stir quickly to prevent the porridge from sticking. Reduce to medium-high heat and cook for 7–8 minutes, or until the porridge reaches the desired consistency. Remove from the heat.

Divide the porridge between 2 bowls. Top with the banana pieces and candied nuts and sprinkle with the toasted pumpkin seeds to serve.

Buckwheat and Oats with Rum, Pineapple, and Amaretti Cookies

Put the buckwheat and oats into a medium pan, pour in the coconut milk and 1½ cups (12 fl oz / 350 ml) water and place over medium heat. Bring to a simmer, cover, and cook for 20 minutes, stirring, or until the porridge reaches the desired consistency. Remove from the heat.

Place a skillet (frying pan) over medium-high heat and add the pineapple. Caramelize the outside of the pineapple for a couple of minutes, then add 1 tablespoon of the rum. Remove from the heat.

Put the amaretti cookies into a small plastic bag, such as a sandwich or freezer bag. Leave the bag open, wrap it in a dish towel, and use a rolling pin to crush the cookies.

Stir the remaining rum into the buckwheat and oats and divide between 2 bowls. Top with the pineapple and the crushed amaretti cookies. Sprinkle with the coconut and drizzle with the maple syrup to serve.

SERVES 2
PREPARATION 3 MIN
COOKING 20 MIN

½ CUP (3 OZ / 85 G) BUCKWHEAT
½ CUP (1½ OZ / 40 G) STEEL-CUT
  OATS (PINHEAD OATMEAL)
1½ CUPS (12 FL OZ / 350 ML)
  COCONUT MILK BEVERAGE
¼ CUP (1 OZ / 25 G) PINEAPPLE
  CHUNKS
3 TABLESPOONS GOOD-QUALITY
  DARK RUM
2 AMARETTI COOKIES
1 TEASPOON GRATED FRESH OR DRY
  SHREDDED (DESICCATED) COCONUT
1 TABLESPOON MAPLE SYRUP

Quinoa, Millet, and Oats with Pear, Chestnut Cream, and Chocolate Sauce

SERVES 2
PREPARATION 5 MIN
COOKING 30 MIN

GENEROUS ½ CUP (2 OZ / 50 G) COOKED
   CHESTNUTS (CANNED OR FROM A JAR)
¼ TEASPOON VANILLA BEAN PASTE
¼ CUP (2 FL OZ / 60 ML)
   HEAVY (DOUBLE) CREAM
1 TEASPOON SUPERFINE
   (CASTER) SUGAR
2¼ OZ / 60 G BITTERSWEET (DARK)
CHOCOLATE (MINIMUM 70%
   COCOA SOLIDS)
5 TABLESPOONS WHIPPING CREAM
½ TEASPOON BUTTER
1 TABLESPOON QUINOA
1 TABLESPOON MILLET
1½ CUPS (12 FL OZ / 350 ML)
   COCONUT MILK BEVERAGE
½ CUP (2 OZ / 50 G) ROLLED OATS
1 PEAR, SLICED

Put the chestnuts, vanilla, cream, and sugar into a small pan and bring to a simmer over medium heat. Cook for 10 minutes, or until the chestnuts are soft. Transfer to a blender or food processor and pulse until you have a smooth chestnut cream. Set aside.

Break the chocolate into small pieces. Put it into a heavy pan with the whipping cream and heat slowly over low heat, stirring occasionally, until the chocolate has melted. Stir until smooth, then stir in the butter. Remove from the heat and set aside.

Put the quinoa and millet into a medium pan, pour in the coconut milk and 1½ cups (12 fl oz / 350 ml) water and place over medium heat. Bring to a simmer, cover, and cook for 20 minutes. Add the oats and increase the heat to medium. Stir until the porridge reaches the desired consistency. You may need to add up to ¼ cup (2 fl oz / 60 ml) more water if most of the liquid has been absorbed. Remove from the heat.

Divide the porridge between 2 bowls. Top with the pear slices, chestnut cream, and chocolate sauce to serve.

Amaranth, Oats, and Kamut with Cherries, White Chocolate, Pistachios, and Chia Seeds

Put the amaranth into a medium pan, pour in the almond milk and 1½ cups (12 fl oz / 350 ml) water and place over high heat. Bring to a boil, cover, and reduce the heat to a simmer. Cook for 15 minutes.

Meanwhile, if using frozen cherries, put them into a small pan with 1 tablespoon water and the sugar, if using. Place over low heat until they have thawed. If using fresh cherries, slice them in half and remove the pits (stones). Set aside.

Add the oats and kamut flakes to the amaranth and increase the heat to medium. You may need to add up to ¼ cup (2 fl oz / 60 ml) more water if the amaranth has absorbed too much liquid. Cook, stirring, for 7 minutes, or until the porridge reaches the desired consistency. Remove from the heat.

Divide the porridge between 2 bowls. Top with the cherries, white chocolate, pistachios, and chia seeds. Dust with the blueberry powder, if using, and drizzle with the maple syrup to serve.

SERVES 2
PREPARATION 3 MIN
COOKING 25 MIN

⅓ CUP (2¼ OZ / 60 G) AMARANTH
1½ CUPS (12 FL OZ / 350 ML)
  ALMOND MILK
6–8 FRESH OR FROZEN CHERRIES
1 TEASPOON SUPERFINE
  (CASTER) SUGAR, (OPTIONAL)
⅓ CUP (1 OZ / 30 G) ROLLED OATS
⅓ CUP (1 OZ / 30 G) KAMUT FLAKES
1 OZ / 25 G WHITE CHOCOLATE,
  CHOPPED
2 TABLESPOONS PISTACHIOS,
  FINELY CHOPPED
1 TEASPOON CHIA SEEDS
½ TEASPOON DRIED BLUEBERRY
  POWDER (OPTIONAL)
1 TABLESPOON MAPLE SYRUP

6-Grain Porridge with Roasted Figs, Wild Honey, Toasted Seeds, and Espresso Cream

Preheat the oven to 350°F/180°C/Gas Mark 4. Line a small baking dish with parchment (baking) paper and set aside.

Cut a cross in the top of each fig. In a bowl mix the honey and sherry, coat the figs in the mixture, then place them in the prepared dish and drizzle any remaining mixture over the top. Cover with aluminum foil and bake for about 20 minutes. Remove from the oven and let cool a little.

Meanwhile, make the cream. In a separate bowl whisk the cream, espresso powder, and sugar together until the mixture holds stiff peaks. Set aside.

Put the mixed grains into a medium pan, pour in the coconut milk beverage and 1½ cups (12 fl oz / 350 ml) water and place over high heat. Bring to a boil. Once the liquid has begun to reduce, stir quickly to prevent the porridge from sticking. Reduce to medium-high heat and cook for 7–8 minutes, or until the porridge reaches the desired consistency. Remove from the heat.

Divide the porridge between 2 bowls. Top with the roasted figs and the espresso cream. Scatter with the toasted seeds to serve.

SERVES 2
PREPARATION 5 MIN
COOKING 20 MIN

4 RIPE FIGS
2 TEASPOONS WILD HONEY
2 TEASPOONS AMONTILLADO SHERRY
2 TABLESPOONS CHILLED
  WHIPPING CREAM
¼ TEASPOON INSTANT ESPRESSO
  POWDER
½ TEASPOON SUPERFINE
  (CASTER) SUGAR
1 CUP (3½ OZ / 100 G) MIXED ROLLED
  OATS, RYE FLAKES, KAMUT FLAKES,
  WHEAT FLAKES, BARLEY FLAKES,
  AND SPELT FLAKES
1½ CUPS (12 FL OZ / 350 ML) COCONUT
  MILK BEVERAGE
2 TABLESPOONS MIX OF TOASTED
  PUMPKIN, SUNFLOWER, CHIA,
  AND SESAME SEEDS

Millet and Quinoa with Blood Orange Curd, Blackberry, and Mascarpone

SERVES 2
PREPARATION 5 MIN,
PLUS CHILLING TIME
COOKING 25 MIN

1 EXTRA-LARGE EGG (UK LARGE)

2 TABLESPOONS SUPERFINE
  (CASTER) SUGAR

½ TEASPOON VANILLA BEAN PASTE

1 TEASPOON FINELY GRATED BLOOD
  ORANGE ZEST

3 TABLESPOONS FRESH BLOOD
  ORANGE JUICE

3 TABLESPOONS FRESH LEMON JUICE

PINCH OF SALT

3 TABLESPOONS UNSALTED
  BUTTER, CUBED

½ CUP (3½ OZ / 100 G) MILLET

⅓ CUP (2¼ OZ / 60 G) QUINOA

1 CUP (8 FL OZ / 250 ML) ALMOND MILK

2 TABLESPOONS MASCARPONE

2 TEASPOONS DRIED BLACKBERRY
  POWDER

In a medium bowl whisk the egg, sugar, and vanilla together until pale and thick. Set aside.

Put the blood orange zest and juice, the lemon juice and salt into a small pan over medium heat and bring it to a simmer. Once simmering, gradually pour in half of the juice mixture to the egg mixture while whisking constantly. Then pour that into the remaining juice mixture in the pan while still whisking constantly. Reduce the heat to medium-low and cook, stirring with a wooden spoon, for about 3 minutes, or until the bubbles subside and the mixture is thick enough to coat the spoon.

Remove from the heat and whisk in the butter, a few pieces at a time. Transfer the resulting curd to a medium bowl and press plastic wrap (clingfilm) directly onto the surface. Let cool and then chill in the refrigerator until cold.

Put the millet and quinoa into a medium pan, pour in the almond milk and 1 cup (8 fl oz / 250 ml) water and place over high heat. Bring to a boil. Reduce to a simmer, cover, and cook for 15 minutes, or until the porridge reaches the desired consistency. Remove from the heat.

Divide the porridge between 2 bowls. Top with the blood orange curd and mascarpone. Dust with blackberry powder to serve.

Quinoa, Oats, and Buckwheat with Oreo Cookies, Frozen Berries, and Salted Caramel

Put the quinoa and buckwheat into a medium pan, pour in the almond milk and 1½ cups (12 fl oz / 350 ml) water and place over high heat. Bring to a boil, cover, and reduce the heat to a simmer. Cook for 20 minutes.

Add the oats to the pan and increase the heat to medium. Cook, stirring, for 8 minutes, or until the porridge reaches the desired consistency. You may need to add up to ¼ cup (2 fl oz / 60 ml) more water if the quinoa has absorbed a lot of liquid. Remove from the heat.

Meanwhile, put the sugar and liquid glucose into a heavy pan and place over medium heat. Heat until the mixture becomes an amber-colored caramel. Do not be tempted to shake the pan or stir the caramel initially.

Gradually pour in the cream and mix well. Remove from the heat and gradually stir in the butter and sea salt.

Divide the porridge between 2 bowls. Top with the cookie pieces and the frozen berries. Drizzle with as much or as little of the salted caramel as desired to serve.

SERVES 2
PREPARATION 5 MIN
COOKING 28 MIN

1 TABLESPOON QUINOA
¼ CUP (1½ OZ / 40 G) BUCKWHEAT
1½ CUPS (12 FL OZ / 350 ML)
   ALMOND MILK
½ CUP (2 OZ / 50 G) ROLLED OATS
2½ TABLESPOONS SUPERFINE
   (CASTER) SUGAR
1 TEASPOON LIQUID GLUCOSE
1½ TABLESPOONS WHIPPING CREAM
2 TABLESPOONS BUTTER, AT
   ROOM TEMPERATURE
PINCH OF SEA SALT
2 OREO COOKIES, BROKEN
   INTO BITE-SIZE PIECES
¼ CUP (1½ OZ / 40 G) FROZEN
   SUMMER OR WINTER BERRIES

5-Grain Porridge with Cranberries, Pecans, and Salted Honeycomb

SERVES 2
PREPARATION 5 MIN
COOKING 20 MIN

1 CUP (3½ OZ / 100 G) CRANBERRIES
1 TABLESPOON PORT (OPTIONAL)
GRATED ZEST AND JUICE OF
   1 ORANGE
2 TABLESPOONS SUPERFINE
   (CASTER) SUGAR
PINCH GROUND CINNAMON
PINCH GROUND CARDAMOM
1 CUP (3½ OZ / 100 G) MIXED ROLLED
   OATS, RYE FLAKES, WHEAT FLAKES,
   BARLEY FLAKES, AND SPELT FLAKES
1½ CUPS (12 FL OZ / 350 ML)
   COCONUT MILK BEVERAGE
1½ TABLESPOONS TOASTED PECANS

FOR THE SALTED HONEYCOMB
¼ CUP + 2 TEASPOONS SUPERFINE
   (CASTER) SUGAR
2 TABLESPOONS MAPLE SYRUP
¾ TABLESPOON BAKING SODA
   (BICARBONATE OF SODA)
⅓ TEASPOON FLAKY SEA SALT

Line a baking sheet with parchment (baking) paper.

To make the salted honeycomb, combine the sugar and maple syrup with 1 tablespoon cold water in a medium heavy pan. Set over medium-high heat and bring the mixture to a boil without stirring. Cook until it reaches 325°F/160°C and is a dark-amber color.

Working quickly, remove the pan from the heat and whisk in the baking soda (bicarbonate of soda). Do not over-whisk it. Immediately pour the mixture onto the lined baking sheet, using a heatproof spatula to scrape it from the pan. Do not smooth the mixture as that will remove the air bubbles from the honeycomb.

Quickly sprinkle the surface evenly with the sea salt, then set the baking sheet in a cool, dry place and allow the honeycomb to cool. Once cool, break it into uneven chunks with your fingers. Set aside.

Combine the cranberries, port, if using, orange zest and juice, sugar, cinnamon, and cardamom in a small pan and bring to a boil. Reduce the heat and simmer for 5–10 minutes, or until the cranberries are tender and the sauce has thickened. Taste, and add more sugar if desired. Stir in the pecans and set aside to cool.

Put the oats, rye flakes, wheat flakes, barley flakes, and spelt flakes into a medium pan, add the coconut milk and 1½ cups (12 fl oz / 350 ml) water and place over high heat. Bring to a boil. Once the liquid has begun to reduce, stir quickly to prevent the porridge from sticking. Reduce to medium-high heat and cook for 8 minutes, or until the porridge reaches the desired consistency. Remove from the heat.

Divide the porridge between 2 bowls. Top with the cranberries, honeycomb chunks, and pecans to serve.

Kamut and Wheat with Apple, Pear, Flaxseed, and Cider Caramel Sauce

Place a medium pan over medium-high heat. Pour in the cider and bring to a boil. Once reduced to 1 tablespoon, quickly add the brown sugar, butter, cream, and cinnamon. Continue to cook until the caramel thickens and starts to become dark in color. Remove from the heat and stir in the vanilla and salt. As it cools, the caramel will thicken.

Put the kamut flakes and wheat flakes into a medium pan, pour in the coconut milk beverage and 1½ cups (12 fl oz / 350 ml) water and place over high heat. Bring to a boil. Once the liquid has begun to reduce, stir quickly to prevent it from sticking. Reduce to medium-high heat and cook for 8–12 minutes, or until the porridge reaches the desired consistency. Remove from the heat.

Divide the kamut and wheat between 2 bowls. Top with the diced pear and the apple matchsticks. Drizzle with as much or as little of the caramel sauce as desired and sprinkle with the flaxseed (linseed) to serve.

SERVES 2
PREPARATION 5 MIN
COOKING 15 MIN

½ CUP (4 FL OZ / 120 ML) HARD
   APPLE CIDER
3 TABLESPOONS LIGHT BROWN
   SUGAR, PACKED
1 TABLESPOON SALTED BUTTER
3 TABLESPOONS HEAVY
   (DOUBLE) CREAM
¼ TEASPOON GROUND CINNAMON
½ TEASPOON VANILLA BEAN PASTE
¼ TEASPOON SEA SALT
½ CUP (2 OZ / 50 G) KAMUT FLAKES
½ CUP (2 OZ / 50 G) WHEAT FLAKES
1½ CUPS (12 FL OZ / 350 ML)
   COCONUT MILK BEVERAGE
1 APPLE, CUT INTO MATCHSTICKS
½ RIPE PEAR, DICED
1 TABLESPOON FLAXSEED (LINSEED)

Buckwheat and Oats with Sesame, Puffed Amaranth, Blackberries, and Clotted Cream

Place a medium pan over medium heat. Add the sesame oil, sesame seeds, puffed amaranth, and sugar. Shake the pan to coat the amaranth. Remove from the heat after 1 minute, or when the amaranth starts to turn golden. Set aside.

Place a small pan over medium heat, add the blackberries and 1 tablespoon water. Allow the fruit to break down a little for 2–3 minutes. Remove from the heat.

Put the buckwheat into a medium pan, pour in the almond milk and 1½ cups (12 fl oz / 350 ml) water and place over high heat. Bring to a simmer, cover and cook for 15 minutes, then add the oats and cook until the porridge reaches the desired consistency. You may need to add ¼ cup (2 fl oz / 60 ml) more water if the buckwheat has absorbed a lot of liquid. Remove from the heat.

Divide the buckwheat and oats between 2 bowls. Top with the blackberries and clotted cream. Scatter with the puffed amaranth and drizzle with the maple syrup to serve.

SERVES 2
PREPARATION 3 MIN
COOKING 20 MIN

1 TEASPOON SESAME OIL
1 TEASPOON SESAME SEEDS
2 TABLESPOONS PUFFED AMARANTH
½ TEASPOON SUPERFINE
   (CASTER) SUGAR
½ CUP (2¾ OZ / 70 G) BLACKBERRIES
½ CUP (3 OZ / 80 G) BUCKWHEAT
1½ CUPS (12 FL OZ / 350 ML)
   ALMOND MILK
½ CUP (2 OZ / 50 G) ROLLED OATS
4 TABLESPOONS CLOTTED CREAM
   OR WHIPPED HEAVY
   (DOUBLE) CREAM
2 TABLESPOONS MAPLE SYRUP

Oats and Kamut with Strawberry Puree, Black Currant Meringue, and Sesame Seeds

Heat the oven to 250°F/120°C/Gas Mark ½. Line a baking sheet with parchment (baking) paper.

Put the black currants into a small pan with 2 teaspoons water. Place over medium heat, bring to a simmer, and cook for 5 minutes, or until soft. Pass the black currants through a strainer (sieve). While they are still warm, sift the confectioners' (icing) sugar into the liquid and stir. Leave to cool completely.

Whisk the egg white until it holds firm peaks. Gradually add the superfine (caster) sugar, 1 teaspoon at a time. You should have a very glossy meringue that holds firm peaks.

Add 1 teaspoon of the black currant puree to the meringue and gently swirl it through to marble it, keeping it nice and streaky. Spoon the meringue into a pastry (piping) bag and pipe 6–8 teardrop shapes onto the prepared baking sheet. Bake for 1½ hours, then leave the meringue in the oven with the door open until the oven has completely cooled.

Put the strawberries into a blender and pulse until you have a puree. Set aside.

Put the oats into a medium pan, pour in the coconut milk and 1½ cups (12 fl oz / 350 ml) water and place over high heat. Bring to a boil, then reduce heat to a simmer, cover, and cook for 15 minutes. Add the kamut flakes and cook for a few more minutes or until the porridge reaches the desired consistency. You may need to add up to ¼ cup (2 fl oz / 60 ml) water if the oats have absorbed a lot of liquid. Remove from the heat.

Divide the oats and kamut between 2 bowls. Top with the meringue teardrops and as much of the strawberry puree and remaining black currant puree as desired. Sprinkle with the sesame seeds and perhaps a crushed meringue, to serve.

SERVES 2
PREPARATION 10 MIN
COOKING 1½ HRS, PLUS COOLING

½ CUP (2 OZ / 50 G) BLACK CURRANTS
1 TEASPOON CONFECTIONERS'
  (ICING) SUGAR
½ EGG WHITE
2 TABLESPOONS SUPERFINE
  (CASTER) SUGAR
½ CUP (2¼ OZ / 60 G)
  STRAWBERRIES, HULLED
SCANT ½ CUP (1½ OZ / 40 G)
  STEEL-CUT OATS (PINHEAD OATMEAL)
½ CUP (2 OZ / 50 G) KAMUT FLAKES
1½ CUPS (12 FL OZ / 350 ML)
  COCONUT MILK BEVERAGE
2 TEASPOONS SESAME SEEDS

4-Grain Porridge with Licorice Summer Fruit Compote, Ginger Snaps, and Coconut

Put the summer fruit into a small pan and place over medium heat. Add 2 tablespoons water. Allow the fruit to cook for 5 minutes, or until soft. Remove from the heat and stir in the sugar and licorice. Set aside.

Put the oats, kamut flakes, wheat flakes, and rye flakes into a medium pan, add the almond milk and 1½ cups (12 fl oz / 350 ml) water and place over high heat. Bring to a boil. Once the liquid has begun to reduce, stir very quickly to prevent the porridge from sticking. Reduce to medium-high heat and cook for 7–8 minutes, or until the porridge reaches the preferred consistency. Remove from the heat.

Divide the porridge between 2 bowls. Top with the summer fruit compote and sprinkle with the crumbled gingersnaps (gingernuts) and coconut to serve.

SERVES 2
PREPARATION 2 MIN
COOKING 10 MIN

½ CUP (3½ OZ / 100 G) FROZEN
  SUMMER FRUIT (STRAWBERRIES,
  RASPBERRIES, BLUEBERRIES)
2 TEASPOONS SUPERFINE
  (CASTER) SUGAR
¼ TEASPOON LICORICE POWDER OR
  1 INCH / 2.5 CM LICORICE STICK
¼ CUP (1 OZ / 25 G) ROLLED OATS
¼ CUP (1 OZ / 25 G) KAMUT FLAKES
¼ CUP (1 OZ / 25 G) WHEAT FLAKES
¼ CUP (1 OZ / 25 G) RYE FLAKES
1½ CUPS (12 FL OZ / 350 ML)
  ALMOND MILK
2 HIGH-QUALITY GINGERSNAPS
  (GINGERNUTS), CRUMBLED
2 TEASPOONS GRATED FRESH OR DRY
  SHREDDED (DESICCATED) COCONUT

Quinoa and Rye with Pistachios, Pears, and Salted Caramel Popcorn

Put the pistachios into a coffee grinder or food processor. Pulse or grind the nuts until you get something that resembles a fine powder but not a paste. (Alternatively you can use a mortar and grind with a pestle.) Reserve 1 teaspoon of the powder for topping the porridge.

Place a skillet (frying pan) over medium heat and add the pear. Allow the slices to brown a little on each side, then remove from the heat.

Put the quinoa into a medium pan, pour in the almond milk and 1¼ cups (10 fl oz / 300 ml) water and place over high heat. Bring to a boil, cover, and reduce the heat to a simmer. Cook for about 15 minutes.

Add the rye flakes and pistachio powder and increase the heat to medium. You may need to add up to ½ cup (4 fl oz / 120 ml) more water if the quinoa absorbs a lot of liquid. Stir until the porridge reaches the desired consistency, then remove from the heat.

Divide the porridge between 2 bowls. Top with the pear slices, then sprinkle with the orange zest, salted caramel popcorn, and the reserved pistachio powder. Spoon the orange juice on top to serve.

SERVES 2
PREPARATION 5 MIN
COOKING 25 MIN

¼ CUP (1 OZ / 25 G)
  SHELLED PISTACHIOS
½ RIPE PEAR, THINLY SLICED
  LENGTHWISE
½ CUP (2¾ OZ / 80 G) QUINOA
1½ CUPS (12 FL OZ / 350 ML)
  ALMOND MILK
½ CUP (2 OZ / 50 G) RYE FLAKES
1 TEASPOON GRATED ORANGE ZEST
4 TABLESPOONS SALTED CARAMEL
  POPCORN
2 TEASPOONS ORANGE JUICE

Put the sugar, cinnamon, and 1 tablespoon water into a small pan over medium-high heat and heat until the sugar has dissolved. Add the almonds and stir constantly with a metal slotted spoon, coating the almonds with the mixture. Stir for about 5 minutes or until the sugar crystalizes. The sugar should look sandy in texture. Remove from the heat and set aside.

Put the oats, barley, and chia seeds into a medium pan. Pour in the coconut milk beverage and 1½ cups (12 fl oz / 350 ml) water and place over high heat. Bring to a boil. Once the liquid has begun to reduce, stir quickly to prevent the porridge from sticking. Reduce to medium-high heat and cook for 5–6 minutes, or until the porridge reaches the desired consistency, then stir in the lemon curd, zest, and maca powder. Remove from the heat.

Divide the porridge between 2 bowls and scatter with the crystalized almonds to serve.

Oats and Barley with Lemon, Chia Seeds, and Crystalized Almonds

SERVES 2
PREPARATION 5 MIN
COOKING 20 MIN

2 TABLESPOONS SUPERFINE
  (CASTER) SUGAR
1 TEASPOON GROUND CINNAMON
½ CUP (2¾ OZ / 70 G) WHOLE
  ALMONDS, RAW BLANCHED
½ CUP (2 OZ / 50 G) ROLLED OATS
½ CUP (2 OZ / 50 G) BARLEY FLAKES
2 TABLESPOONS CHIA SEEDS
1½ CUPS (12 FL OZ / 350 ML) COCONUT
  MILK BEVERAGE
4 TABLESPOONS LEMON CURD
1 TEASPOON GRATED LEMON ZEST
1 TEASPOON MACA POWDER

Quinoa, Barley, and Spelt with Roasted Pineapple, Long Pepper, and Mango

Preheat the oven to 350°F/180°C/Gas Mark 4. Line a baking sheet with parchment (baking) paper.

Put the pineapple chunks on the prepared baking sheet, then drizzle with the honey. Bake for 25 minutes, remove from the oven, and set aside.

Meanwhile, put the mango, long pepper, stevia or superfine (caster) sugar, and 2 tablespoons water into a small pan. Place over medium heat and cook for 5 minutes. Remove from the heat, remove the long pepper, and set aside.

Put the quinoa into a medium pan, pour in the coconut milk beverage and 1½ cups (12 fl oz / 350 ml) water and place over medium-low heat. Bring to a simmer, cover, and cook for 15 minutes. Add the barley and spelt and increase the heat to medium. You may need to add up to ¼ cup (2 fl oz / 60 ml) water if the quinoa has absorbed a lot of liquid. Stir until the porridge reaches the desired consistency. Remove from the heat.

Divide the porridge between 2 bowls. Top with the pineapple and mango. Spoon on the crème fraîche and sprinkle with the flaked almonds to serve.

SERVES 2
PREPARATION 5 MIN
COOKING 25 MIN

½ CUP (2¼ OZ / 60 G)
  PINEAPPLE CHUNKS
2 TEASPOONS HONEY
½ MANGO, CHOPPED INTO CHUNKS
1 STICK OF LONG PEPPER OR 5 WHOLE
  BLACK PEPPERCORNS
¼ TEASPOON STEVIA OR 2 TEASPOONS
  SUPERFINE (CASTER) SUGAR
⅓ CUP (2¼ OZ / 60 G) QUINOA
1½ CUPS (12 FL OZ / 350 ML)
  COCONUT MILK BEVERAGE
¼ CUP (1 OZ / 25 G) BARLEY FLAKES
¼ CUP (1 OZ / 25 G) SPELT FLAKES
1 TABLESPOON CRÈME FRAÎCHE
1 TABLESPOON TOASTED
  FLAKED ALMONDS

Glossary

Glossary

ACAI BERRY PULP Frozen organic Acai berries come from the acai palm, which is native to Central and South America where they are prized for their nutritional value. They are ground into a pulp and then frozen so the pulp can be easily used in drinks and other liquids. It has a deep fruity, almost chocolate flavor, and is packed with antioxidants and vitamins to support the immune system, plus essential omega fatty acids.

ALMOND MILK A plant milk made from almonds and water, when homemade. It has a creamy texture and a slightly nutty taste. It is lactose free and as such is often used as a substitute for cow's milk by people who are lactose-intolerant or vegan. There are now commercial brands that produce fresh almond milk, which is sold in grocery stores, super-markets as well as specialist health-food stores.

AMARANTH A grain of South American origin, consumed by the Aztecs so it is referred to as an ancient grain. It is a very small grain in comparison to oats or other rolled/flaked grains like barley and rye. It can have a gelatinous texture when cooked without any other grains to accompany it. It is gluten free.

AMARANTH, PUFFED Amaranth grain that has been par-boiled and then dried in an oven to make it puff up like popcorn.

AMARENA CHERRIES Specifically grown in Bologna and Modena in Italy, these small, rather bitter cherries are usually found bottled in syrup.

BARLEY FLAKES Barley is considered a whole grain, commonly associated with beer and whiskey production. Flaked or rolled barley has a more delicate texture and flavor in comparison to other whole grains.

BEE POLLEN These are the pollen balls produced by bees, which are small and yellow in color. They are sold as a health food product. Do not eat bee pollen if you are pregnant, breastfeeding, following a vegan diet, or if you have experienced pollen allergies.

BLACK RICE Black rice, like brown rice is highly nutritious when compared to white rice. It has high levels of antioxidants, iron and vitamin E. It has a mild, nutty flavor. It is gluten free.

BLACKBERRY POWDER Blackberries are dried and ground into a powder. The powder is enormously nutritious and can be added to smoothies and yogurt or sprinkled onto desserts or a bowl of cooked grains.

BLOOD SAUSAGE Known as blood pudding or black pudding. It is actually mostly made up of oats and spices with pig's blood being used to set the ingredients together. Delicious fried in slices.

BLUEBERRY POWDER Blueberries are dried and ground into a powder. Packed full of antioxidants, vitamins, and nutrients the powder can be added to smoothies and yogurt or sprinkled onto desserts or a bowl of cooked grains.

BRANDY SNAP A baked sweet snack, which is characterized by being a thin disk, molded into a tubular form. They are often filled with cream and resemble cannoli in appearance and shape. They are closely related to gingerbread in terms of flavor.

BUCKWHEAT Despite its name, buckwheat is not related to wheat. It is rich in complex carbohydrates. It is gluten free

Cacao nibs, raw The raw form of chocolate before it is processed and the heart of the cocoa bean. Once cocoa beans are fermented, dried, and roasted, the shells are removed and the nibs are exposed. Very crunchy and with a bitter chocolate flavor—they are unsweetened—raw cacao nibs can be finely chopped, crushed, or even ground to a powder and used to give a rich cocoa flavor.

Chia seeds Seeds from the chia plant. The plant has small blue flowers and is part of the mint family and native to the southwestern US and Mexico. The flowers and the edible seeds are highly nutritious and used for food and drinks. Now widely used in raw and health food recipes, these nutritious blackish-gray, poppy seed-size grains swell greatly when soaked in liquid, acting as a helpful thickening ingredient. Grinding or crushing the seeds before use helps the body to digest chia.

Chimichurri sauce A green sauce originally from Argentina that is often served with grilled meats. The primary ingredients are parsley, garlic, oregano, cilantro (coriander), chili, vegetable oil, and white vinegar.

Coconut milk beverage Not to be confused with coconut milk in a can, new brands now sell milk made from coconuts. It is sold in cartons and can be found in the milk aisle at specialist health food stores and at some supermarkets.

Cranberry powder Cranberries are dried and ground into a powder. The powder is very tart and enormously nutritious. It can be added to smoothies and yogurt or sprinkled onto desserts or a bowl of cooked grains to add tartness.

Elderflower cordial Syrup made from sugar, water, and the cream-colored flowers of the elderberry tree. Elderflowers flower at the start of the summer, and have a short season.

Espresso powder Ground coffee beans used to make espresso coffee.

Flaxseed Also known as linseed, these are seeds from any plant of the genus Linum. The plants are slender, have lance-shaped leaves and blue flowers. The seeds are rich in fiber and magnesium. They can be eaten whole but for easier digestion and better absorption, grind flaxseeds before use (then keep in the refrigerator and use within a week).

Gingersnaps Also known as gingernuts, they are cookies flavored with powdered ginger and a variety of other spices, most commonly cinnamon, molasses, and nutmeg.

Girolle Also known as a golden chanterelle, this delicious mushroom is characterized by the fact that it smells sweet, like apricots, when in season. Trumpet-shaped and orangey-yellow in appearance, with a slightly chewy texture, it imparts a rich nutty flavor to many dishes.

Goat curd This is the curd produced by goat milk when rennet is added to separate the curds from the whey. It is a delicious mild cheese that is lower in lactose content than cow's milk.

Goji berries These small, shriveled, reddish orange berries are cultivated in China and have a slightly sweet but herbal taste. They are highly nutritious. High in antioxidants, they can easily be found in all health food stores and some grocery stores and supermarkets. Normally sold in dried form, you can sprinkle them over breakfast, into smoothies, or yogurt.

Greengages These are a group of historically European plums; they are however grown in other territories too. They range in color from dark green to yellow. Sweet and very juicy with a soft, delicate, aromatic flesh, greengages are at their best when eaten raw.

Glossary

HAZELNUT MILK Plant milk made from hazelnuts and water, when homemade. It has a creamy texture and a nutty taste. It is lactose free and as such is can be used as a substitute for cow's milk by people who are lactose-intolerant or vegan. Commercial brands can be found in specialist health-food stores.

HONEY, WILD Any honey produced by wild bees with hives in trees, rocks, and anywhere not in a commercial bee hive.

KAMUT FLAKES Kamut is also known as Khorasan wheat and is of Arabic and Asian origin. It is a delicious nutty flavored alternative to wheat.

KINDER SCHOCKO-BONS Made by the candy brand Kinder, these bite-size, egg-shape chocolates have a milky center that contains hazelnut pieces. The eggs are then coated in fine milk chocolate.

KIRSCH A sweet brandy made from the distillation of sour cherries. It is clear in color.

KOHLRABI Also known as a German turnip, it is green or purple in color and part of the cabbage family of plants. It resembles a turnip or swede in appearance.

LIQUID GLUCOSE Thick syrup made primarily of dextrose with dextrins, maltose, and water. It is used in caramel to make it more fluid at lower temperatures or in icing to keep it soft.

LICORICE POWDER Made from the root of the plant Glycyrrhiza glabra, this powder is used to make licorice sweets and can be added to sweet or savory dishes to provide an aniseed flavor.

LONG PEPPER Sometimes known as Indian long pepper and is usually dried and used as a spice. Black pepper is a close alternative.

MILKA DAIM BAR Made by the candy brand Milka, this confection combines Milka chocolate with Daim—a crunchy almond caramel.

MILLET Largely grown in Asia and Africa this is one of the smaller grains but rich in protein and vitamins. It is gluten free.

MOREL MUSHROOMS A highly celebrated mushroom known for its distinctive flavor. Its conical cap is pitted with a honeycomb of small deep holes so it is essential to clean it carefully in several changes of water. Dark-capped morels, that are brownish-black in color, are the most sought after, while 'blonde' morels are less rare. It is essential to ensure they are fully cooked to remove the toxic substances they contain.

OATS, JUMBO Large rolled oats. Cereal and breakfast brands sieve out the larger oats to be sold as a separate product. These are more difficult to find in North America but can easily be substituted with rolled oats.

OATS, REGULAR ROLLED The rolled or flaked version of oats. Oats are rich in protein, minerals, and vitamins. They are the most common grain used for oatmeal (porridge).

OATS, STEEL CUT Also known as pinhead oatmeal, these are whole oat grains that have been cut into two or three pieces. They take longer than rolled oats to cook.

PEA SHOOTS The leaves of a young pea plant. Rich in vitamin C, A, and protein, with a light pea flavor, they are perfect to garnish a grain bowl and are delicious in salads.

PEARLED BARLEY Barley is considered a whole grain, commonly associated with beer and whiskey production. The process to pearl the barley grain involves removing the hull and using steam to remove the bran.

PEARLED ITALIAN FARRO Also called pearled spelt, farro is very closely related to wheat and is high in nutritional value. The process to pearl the barley spelt involves removing the hull and using steam to remove the bran. It has a nutty flavor.

Quinoa Often referred to as a grain, quinoa is actually a seed from a vegetable related to Swiss chard, spinach, and beets (beetroot). Regarded as a modern superfood because of its high fiber and protein content and nutritional value, it is gluten free. It has a natural soapy coating known as saponin, a naturally occurring toxin, so it should always be rinsed thoroughly before being used.

Rye flakes Rye is often used as an ingredient for making bread and, in some cases, whiskey and vodka. However, when the grain is flaked, it makes a delicious alternative to oats.

Sea buckthorn powder Sea buckthorn berries are small, orange, and typically grow on sandy coasts. They have a tart, lemony flavor similar to that of a passion fruit. The nutritious berries are dried and ground to make a powder, which can be added to smoothies and yogurt, or sprinkled onto desserts or a bowl of cooked grains.

Sour cherries A species of cherry closely related to the sweet cherry but higher in nutritional value and with a distinctive sour flavor. You can buy them fresh or dried. They work well in savory dishes as well as in jams, jellies, cakes, or sprinkled on top of a hot bowl of porridge.

Spelt flakes Spelt is very closely related to wheat, it is high in nutritional value. When it is flaked it is a lot quicker to cook than pearled Italian farro (pearled spelt).

Star anise This spice is characterized by its eight-pointed star shape and similarity in flavor to anise, which is an unrelated plant. It works well in both sweet and savory dishes.

Stevia Stevia is a sweetener, extracted from the stevia leaf. Although it is still a highly processed product, it does come from a natural source. Significantly sweeter than sugar, it can be bought in granulated or liquid form.

Vanilla bean paste A paste made from the seeds taken from vanilla pods (beans). It is a cost effective alternative to buying vanilla pods and convenient too, because you simply scoop it out of a jar with a teaspoon.

Walnuts, pickled Walnuts that have been picked early, while they are still green, put into a salt brine, drained, left to dry, and then put in jars with more brine. They are considered a delicacy.

Wheat flakes Probably the most recognized grain, after rice and corn. It is more commonly used to make flour. However, flaked wheat is a whole grain and highly nutritious.

Suppliers

UNITED STATES

WORLD MARKET
www.worldmarket.com
Grocery stores and website stocking a range of international food and drink products.

D'ARTAGNAN
www.dartagnan.com
Supplier of free-range meat, poultry, and mushrooms from farms around the world.

BOB'S RED MILL
www.bobsredmill.com
Producer and supplier of whole grains and whole-grain products.

SCOTTISH GOURMET USA
www.scottishgourmetusa.com
Supplier of blood sausage (black pudding), marmalades, and a range of other Scottish delicacies.

MAPLE LEAF FARMS
www.mapleleaffarms.com
Supplier of a range of duck products from family-owned American farms.

IGOURMET.COM
www.igourmet.com
Supplies a large range of fine and gourmet foods and delicacies, including meat, oil, honey, coffee, grains, and condiments.

MOUNTAIN ROSE HERBS
www.mountainroseherbs.com
Supplies a wide range of health powders and seeds.

LIVE SUPERFOODS
www.livesuperfoods.com
Supplier of raw and vegan superfoods, including powders.

WHOLE FOODS MARKET
www.wholefoodsmarket.com
Health-food stores stocking organic produce, delicacies, and superfoods.

NUTS.COM
nuts.com
Supplier of organic nuts, seeds, dried fruits, powders, and grains.

AMAZON
www.amazon.com
Supplier of many hard-to-find food products.

EDEN FOODS
www.edenfoods.com
Supplier of a range of cereal flakes in raw form.

AUSTRALIA

HONEST TO GOODNESS
www.goodness.com.au
Delivers organic food and natural food products, including grains and powders.

AUSSIE HEALTH
www.aussiehealthproducts.com.au
Online health store that delivers organic, gluten-free, and healthy food products, including grains.

KOMBU WHOLEFOODS
www.kombuwholefoods.com.au
Health-food store and online retailer of organic and healthy-living foods.

GOURMET GROCER ONLINE
www.gourmetgroceronline.com.au
Delivers a wide range of gourmet foods and delicacies, including fruit powders.

THE SOURCE BULK FOODS

www.thesourcebulkfoods.com.au
Store and website providing
health foods, including seeds,
powders, nuts, and dried fruit
in reduced packaging.

THE GERMAN SHOP

www.thegermanshop.com.au
Delivers German chocolates
and sweet treats.

HEALTHY LIFE

www.healthylife.net.au
Superstore chain that stocks
organic whole foods and
superfoods.

THE ESSENTIAL INGREDIENT

www.essentialingredient.com.au
Delivers luxury and unique
ingredients, including oil,
mushrooms, and preserves.

UNITED KINGDOM

HOLLAND & BARRETT

www.hollandandbarrett.com
Chain stocking health food
and organic wholefoods
and superfoods.

HEALTHY SUPPLIES

www.healthysupplies.co.uk
Stock a range of cereal flakes
in raw form, dried fruits,
nuts, seeds and gluten free
products.

BUY WHOLEFOODS ONLINE

www.buywholefoodsonline.co.uk
Stocks a range of organic
products across a range of
different food groups.

AMAZON UK

www.amazon.co.uk
Online supplier of many
hard-to-find food products.

ALL THINGS LIQUORICE

www.allthingsliquorice.co.uk
Supplier of licorice powder.

INDIA TREE

www.indiatree.com
Supplier of specialty spices,
herbs, and seeds.

STEENBERGS

www.steenbergs.co.uk
Supplier of organic spices
and herbs.

NISBETS

www.nisbets.co.uk
Suppliers of
kitchen equipment.

WORLDWIDE

BRIT SUPERSTORE

www.britsuperstore.com
Delivers British food products,
drinks, and brands.

Index

ACKNOWLEDGEMENTS

There are many turns of fate that brought this book to life, and I am thankful that they did. Without the tremendous support of my parents, Ian Williamson and Daniela Williamson, along with my mother's long-suffering partner Serif Fateh, I would not have been able to open the Porridge Café, which I can honestly say made this book possible.

I would like to give a special mention to Eleanor Harrington for tireless hours of dedication; for over 400 working hours of toil in one fantastic month in March 2015; for constant inspiration; and for believing in me. She also contributed a great deal to the development of the recipes for this book. You were my partner both in crime and in porridge.

This also leads me to thank Mike and Patsy, your help got us through many days, so thank you for your time and patience.

Many friends helped with offers of free labour and, in many cases, their taste buds, to ensure the recipes were at least edible.

A big thankyou to Maxine, Scarlett, and Rufus who's hands are dotted throughout the pages of the book.

Thank you also to Robert, who spotted me in an article and made the phone call to ask if I would like to make this book. Your enthusiasm was infectious and your efforts have not been in vain.

Thank you to Ellie Smith and Liz Clinton for being patient with me and also pushing me—writing doesn't come naturally to me, so thanks for your help. Thanks to Sam Wolfson and Dan Adams for designing the book and to Sophie Hodgkin for making sure my writing doesn't make me look like a 10 year old.

Thank you to the photographer Andy Sewell and to Pene Parker who came and helped to plate the recipes, along with all the hand models who made this book come to life.

RECIPE NOTES

Unless otherwise stated, individual vegetables and fruits, such as onions and apples, are assumed to be medium.

All herbs are fresh, unless otherwise specified.

Cooking and dehydrating times are for guidance only, as individual ovens and dehydrators vary. If using a convection (fan) oven, follow the manufacturer's instructions concerning oven temperatures.

Exercise a high level of caution when following recipes involving any potentially hazardous activity, including the use of high temperatures and open flames.

Some nut-free recipes include coconut, coconut products, and/or pine nuts. The coconut is classified as a dry drupe, while the brown, fibrous coconut is its seed. Pine nuts, meanwhile, are actually seeds, and so may be safe for some people with a tree nut allergy to eat. Some individuals are allergic to these foods without being allergic to tree nuts; people with nut allergies may also suffer from additional allergies to coconuts or pine nuts. If you have a tree nut allergy, it is best to exercise caution with these foods and consult your doctor.

Some recipes include bee pollen. These should be avoided by pregnant and breastfeeding women, and anyone who has experienced pollen allergies.

Some recipes include raw or very lightly cooked eggs and fermented products. These should be avoided by the elderly, infants, pregnant women, convalescents, and anyone with an impaired immune system.

When no quantity is specified, for example of oils, salts, and herbs used for finishing dishes, quantities are discretionary and flexible.

All herbs, shoots, flowers, berries, and leaves should be picked fresh from a clean source. Exercise caution when foraging for ingredients; any foraged ingredients should only be eaten if an expert has deemed them safe to eat.

Both metric and imperial measures are used in this book. Follow one set of measurements throughout, not a mixture, as they are not interchangeable.

All spoon and cup measurements are level, unless otherwise stated. 1 teaspoon = 5 ml; 1 tablespoon = 15 ml.

Australian standard tablespoons are 20 ml, so Australian readers are advised to use 3 teaspoons in place of 1 tablespoon when measuring small quantities.

Phaidon Press Limited
Regent's Wharf
All Saints Street
London N1 9PA

Phaidon Press Inc.
65 Bleecker Street
New York, NY 10012

www.phaidon.com

First published 2016
© 2016 Phaidon Press Limited

ISBN 978 0 7148 7225 4

A CIP catalogue record for this book is available from the British Library and the Library of Congress.

Commissioning Editor
Ellie Smith

Project Editors
Elizabeth Clinton and
Sophie Hodgkin

Production Controller
Amanda Mackie

Design by BLOK
www.blokdesign.co.uk

Photography
Andy Sewell

The publisher would like to thank Jamie Ambrose, Adrienne Anderson, Vanessa Bird, Maxine Brady, Scarlett Brady, Serif Fateh, Diane Fortenberry, Jan Fullwood, Naomi James, Hannah Kaspar, Vishwa Kaushal, Leonie Kellman, Shahid Mahmood, Sami Mahmood, Virginia McLeod, João Mota, Laura Nickoll, Robert Gwyn Palmer, Pene Parker, Jana Polakova, Tilly Slight, Tracey Smith, Hans Stofregen, and Zek Tahir for their contributions to the book.

Printed in China